ICISS

THE RESPONSIBILITY TO PROTECT

DECEMBER 2001

REPORT OF THE
INTERNATIONAL COMMISSION ON INTERVENTION
AND STATE SOVEREIGNTY

8908564

INTERNATIONAL COMMISSION ON INTERVENTION AND STATE SOVEREIGNTY

Published by the International Development Research Centre
PO Box 8500, Ottawa, ON, Canada K1G 3H9
http://www.idrc.ca

National Library of Canada cataloguing in publication data

International Commission on Intervention and State Sovereignty

The Responsibility to Protect
Report of the International Commission on Intervention and State Sovereignty

Issued also in French under title: *La responsabilité de protéger*.
Issued by the International Development Research Centre.
Accompanied by CD-ROM.

ISBN 0-88936-960-7

1. Intervention (International law).
2. Sovereignty.
3. Security, international.
4. United Nations. Security Council.
5. Humanitarian assistance.
I.   International Development Research Centre (Canada).
II. Title.

JZ6368.I57 2001   327.1′7   C2001-980327-3

IDRC Books endeavours to produce environmentally friendly publications. All paper used
is recycled as well as recyclable. All inks and coatings are vegetable-based products. The
full catalogue of IDRC Books is available at http://www.idrc.ca/booktique.

TABLE OF CONTENTS

FOREWORD

This report is about the so-called "right of humanitarian intervention": the question of when, if ever, it is appropriate for states to take coercive – and in particular military – action, against another state for the purpose of protecting people at risk in that other state. At least until the horrifying events of 11 September 2001 brought to center stage the international response to terrorism, the issue of intervention for human protection purposes has been seen as one of the most controversial and difficult of all international relations questions. With the end of the Cold War, it became a live issue as never before. Many calls for intervention have been made over the last decade – some of them answered and some of them ignored. But there continues to be disagreement as to whether, if there is a right of intervention, how and when it should be exercised, and under whose authority.

The Policy Challenge

External military intervention for human protection purposes has been controversial both when it has happened – as in Somalia, Bosnia and Kosovo – and when it has failed to happen, as in Rwanda. For some the new activism has been a long overdue internationalization of the human conscience; for others it has been an alarming breach of an international state order dependent on the sovereignty of states and the inviolability of their territory. For some, again, the only real issue is ensuring that coercive interventions are effective; for others, questions about legality, process and the possible misuse of precedent loom much larger.

NATO's intervention in Kosovo in 1999 brought the controversy to its most intense head. Security Council members were divided; the legal justification for military action without new Security Council authority was asserted but largely unargued; the moral or humanitarian justification for the action, which on the face of it was much stronger, was clouded by allegations that the intervention generated more carnage than it averted; and there were many criticisms of the way in which the NATO allies conducted the operation.

At the United Nations General Assembly in 1999, and again in 2000, Secretary-General Kofi Annan made compelling pleas to the international community to try to find, once and for all, a new consensus on how to approach these issues, to "forge unity" around the basic questions of principle and process involved. He posed the central question starkly and directly:

> …if humanitarian intervention is, indeed, an unacceptable assault on sovereignty, how should we respond to a Rwanda, to a Srebrenica – to gross and systematic violations of human rights that affect every precept of our common humanity?

It was in response to this challenge that the Government of Canada, together with a group of major foundations, announced at the General Assembly in September 2000 the establishment of the International Commission on Intervention and State Sovereignty (ICISS). Our Commission was asked to wrestle with the whole range of questions – legal, moral, operational and political – rolled up in this debate, to consult with the widest possible range of opinion around the world, and to bring back a report that would help the Secretary-General and everyone else find some new common ground.

The Commission's Report

The report which we now present has been unanimously agreed by the twelve Commissioners. Its central theme, reflected in the title, is "The Responsibility to Protect", the idea that sovereign states have a responsibility to protect their own citizens from avoidable catastrophe – from mass murder and rape, from starvation – but that when they are unwilling or unable to do so, that responsibility must be borne by the broader community of states. The nature and dimensions of that responsibility are argued out, as are all the questions that must be answered about who should exercise it, under whose authority, and when, where and how. We hope very much that the report will break new ground in a way that helps generate a new international consensus on these issues. It is desperately needed.

As Co-Chairs we are indebted to our fellow Commissioners for the extraordinary qualities of knowledge, experience and judgement they brought to the preparation of this report over a long and gruelling year of meetings. The Commissioners brought many different personal views to the table, and the report on which we have agreed does not reflect in all respects the preferred views of any one of them. In particular, some of our members preferred a wider range of threshold criteria for military intervention than those proposed in our report, and others a narrower range. Again, some Commissioners preferred more, and others less, flexibility for military intervention outside the scope of Security Council approval.

But the text on which we have found consensus does reflect the shared views of all Commissioners as to what is politically achievable in the world as we know it today. We want no more Rwandas, and we believe that the adoption of the proposals in our report is the best way of ensuring that. We share a belief that it is critical to move the international consensus forward, and we know that we cannot begin to achieve that if we cannot find consensus among ourselves. We simply hope that what we have achieved can now be mirrored in the wider international community.

The Report and the Events of 11 September 2001

The Commission's report was largely completed before the appalling attacks of 11 September 2001 on New York and Washington DC, and was not conceived as addressing the kind of challenge posed by such attacks. Our report has aimed at providing precise guidance for states faced with human protection claims in other states; it has not been framed to guide the policy of states when faced with attack on their own nationals, or the nationals of other states residing within their borders.

The two situations in our judgement are fundamentally different. The framework the Commission, after consultations around the world, has developed to address the first case (coping with human protection claims in other states) must not be confused with the framework necessary to deal with the second (responding to terrorist attacks in one's own state). Not the least of the differences is that in the latter case the UN Charter provides much more explicit authority for a military response than in the case of intervention for human protection purposes: Article 51 acknowledges "the inherent right of individual or collective self-defence if an armed attack occurs against a Member of the United Nations", though requiring that the measures taken be immediately reported to the Security Council. In Resolutions 1368 and 1373, passed unanimously in the aftermath of the September attacks, the Security Council left no doubt as to the scope of measures that states could and should take in response.

While for the reasons stated we have not – except in passing – addressed in the body of our report the issues raised by the 11 September attacks, there are aspects of our report which do have some relevance to the issues with which the international community has been grappling in the aftermath of those attacks. In particular, the precautionary principles outlined in our report do seem to be relevant to military operations, both multilateral and unilateral, against the scourge of terrorism. We have no difficulty in principle with focused military action being taken against international terrorists and those who harbour them. But military power should always be exercised in a principled way, and the principles of right intention, last resort, proportional means and reasonable prospects outlined in our report are, on the face of it, all applicable to such action.

Acknowledgements

The research and consultations on which the Commission report is based, and the way in which we went about our task, are described in detail in the accompanying supplementary volume, titled *"Research, Bibliography, Background"*. We are indebted to former Canadian Foreign Affairs Minister Lloyd Axworthy, who initiated the Commission and chaired our Advisory Board, and to his successor John Manley who carried it through; to our Canadian support team, headed by Jill Sinclair and Heidi Hulan, for their boundless enthusiasm and energy; and to our research team, headed by Thomas Weiss and Stanlake Samkange, for their dedication and wise counsel. Our work has also benefited profoundly from that of many others who have researched and published on the many different issues on which this report touches, and we acknowledge that contribution more fully in the supplementary volume. We have not tried to reproduce in our report work which has been well and fully done elsewhere – for example on the subject of prevention or operational issues – but we are profoundly conscious of the many debts we owe.

We particularly want to emphasize the benefit we derived from the series of lengthy roundtable discussions we conducted in Beijing, Cairo, Geneva, London, Maputo, New Delhi, New York, Ottawa, Paris, St Petersburg, Santiago and Washington. The meetings involved representatives from governments and inter-governmental organizations, from non-governmental organizations and civil society, and from universities, research institutes and think tanks – in all, over 200 people. These roundtable meetings proved to be a wonderfully rich source of information, ideas and diverse political perspectives, and an excellent real world environment in which the Commission could test its own ideas as they evolved. If we have in our report succeeded in breaking new ground, finding new and constructive ways to tackle the long-standing policy dilemmas associated with intervention for human protection purposes, there are a great many others who can justly claim a share of that success.

GARETH EVANS
MOHAMED SAHNOUN
Co-Chairs
30 September 2001

SYNOPSIS

THE RESPONSIBILITY TO PROTECT: CORE PRINCIPLES

(1) BASIC PRINCIPLES

A. State sovereignty implies responsibility, and the primary responsibility for the protection of its people lies with the state itself.

B. Where a population is suffering serious harm, as a result of internal war, insurgency, repression or state failure, and the state in question is unwilling or unable to halt or avert it, the principle of non-intervention yields to the international responsibility to protect.

(2) FOUNDATIONS

The foundations of the responsibility to protect, as a guiding principle for the international community of states, lie in:

A. obligations inherent in the concept of sovereignty;

B. the responsibility of the Security Council, under Article 24 of the UN Charter, for the maintenance of international peace and security;

C. specific legal obligations under human rights and human protection declarations, covenants and treaties, international humanitarian law and national law;

D. the developing practice of states, regional organizations and the Security Council itself.

(3) ELEMENTS

The responsibility to protect embraces three specific responsibilities:

A. **The responsibility to prevent:** to address both the root causes and direct causes of internal conflict and other man-made crises putting populations at risk.

B. **The responsibility to react:** to respond to situations of compelling human need with appropriate measures, which may include coercive measures like sanctions and international prosecution, and in extreme cases military intervention.

C. **The responsibility to rebuild:** to provide, particularly after a military intervention, full assistance with recovery, reconstruction and reconciliation, addressing the causes of the harm the intervention was designed to halt or avert.

(4) PRIORITIES

A. **Prevention is the single most important dimension of the responsibility to protect:** prevention options should always be exhausted before intervention is contemplated, and more commitment and resources must be devoted to it.

B. The exercise of the responsibility to both prevent and react should always involve less intrusive and coercive measures being considered before more coercive and intrusive ones are applied.

THE RESPONSIBILITY TO PROTECT: PRINCIPLES FOR MILITARY INTERVENTION

(1) THE JUST CAUSE THRESHOLD

Military intervention for human protection purposes is an exceptional and extraordinary measure. To be warranted, there must be serious and irreparable harm occurring to human beings, or imminently likely to occur, of the following kind:

A. **large scale loss of life,** actual or apprehended, with genocidal intent or not, which is the product either of deliberate state action, or state neglect or inability to act, or a failed state situation; or

B. **large scale 'ethnic cleansing'**, actual or apprehended, whether carried out by killing, forced expulsion, acts of terror or rape.

(2) THE PRECAUTIONARY PRINCIPLES

A. **Right intention:** The primary purpose of the intervention, whatever other motives intervening states may have, must be to halt or avert human suffering. Right intention is better assured with multilateral operations, clearly supported by regional opinion and the victims concerned.

B. **Last resort:** Military intervention can only be justified when every non-military option for the prevention or peaceful resolution of the crisis has been explored, with reasonable grounds for believing lesser measures would not have succeeded.

C. **Proportional means:** The scale, duration and intensity of the planned military intervention should be the minimum necessary to secure the defined human protection objective.

D. **Reasonable prospects:** There must be a reasonable chance of success in halting or averting the suffering which has justified the intervention, with the consequences of action not likely to be worse than the consequences of inaction.

(3) RIGHT AUTHORITY

A. There is no better or more appropriate body than the United Nations Security Council to authorize military intervention for human protection purposes. The task is not to find alternatives to the Security Council as a source of authority, but to make the Security Council work better than it has.

B. Security Council authorization should in all cases be sought prior to any military intervention action being carried out. Those calling for an intervention should formally request such authorization, or have the Council raise the matter on its own initiative, or have the Secretary-General raise it under Article 99 of the UN Charter.

C. The Security Council should deal promptly with any request for authority to intervene where there are allegations of large scale loss of human life or ethnic cleansing. It should in this context seek adequate verification of facts or conditions on the ground that might support a military intervention.

D. The Permanent Five members of the Security Council should agree not to apply their veto power, in matters where their vital state interests are not involved, to obstruct the passage of resolutions authorizing military intervention for human protection purposes for which there is otherwise majority support.

E. If the Security Council rejects a proposal or fails to deal with it in a reasonable time, alternative options are:

I. consideration of the matter by the General Assembly in Emergency Special Session under the "Uniting for Peace" procedure; and

II. action within area of jurisdiction by regional or sub-regional organizations under Chapter VIII of the Charter, subject to their seeking subsequent authorization from the Security Council.

F. The Security Council should take into account in all its deliberations that, if it fails to discharge its responsibility to protect in conscience-shocking situations crying out for action, concerned states may not rule out other means to meet the gravity and urgency of that situation – and that the stature and credibility of the United Nations may suffer thereby.

(4) OPERATIONAL PRINCIPLES

A. Clear objectives; clear and unambiguous mandate at all times; and resources to match.

B. Common military approach among involved partners; unity of command; clear and unequivocal communications and chain of command.

C. Acceptance of limitations, incrementalism and gradualism in the application of force, the objective being protection of a population, not defeat of a state.

D. Rules of engagement which fit the operational concept; are precise; reflect the principle of proportionality; and involve total adherence to international humanitarian law.

E. Acceptance that force protection cannot become the principal objective.

F. Maximum possible coordination with humanitarian organizations.

1. THE POLICY CHALLENGE

THE INTERVENTION DILEMMA

1.1 "Humanitarian intervention" has been controversial both when it happens, and when it has failed to happen. Rwanda in 1994 laid bare the full horror of inaction. The United Nations (UN) Secretariat and some permanent members of the Security Council knew that officials connected to the then government were planning genocide; UN forces were present, though not in sufficient number at the outset; and credible strategies were available to prevent, or at least greatly mitigate, the slaughter which followed. But the Security Council refused to take the necessary action. That was a failure of international will – of civic courage – at the highest level. Its consequence was not merely a humanitarian catastrophe for Rwanda: the genocide destabilized the entire Great Lakes region and continues to do so. In the aftermath, many African peoples concluded that, for all the rhetoric about the universality of human rights, some human lives end up mattering a great deal less to the international community than others.

1.2 Kosovo – where intervention *did* take place in 1999 – concentrated attention on all the other sides of the argument. The operation raised major questions about the legitimacy of military intervention in a sovereign state. Was the cause just: were the human rights abuses committed or threatened by the Belgrade authorities sufficiently serious to warrant outside involvement? Did those seeking secession manipulate external intervention to advance their political purposes? Were all peaceful means of resolving the conflict fully explored? Did the intervention receive appropriate authority? How could the bypassing and marginalization of the UN system, by "a coalition of the willing" acting without Security Council approval, possibly be justified? Did the way in which the intervention was carried out in fact worsen the very human rights situation it was trying to rectify? Or – against all this – was it the case that had the North Atlantic Treaty Organization (NATO) not intervened, Kosovo would have been at best the site of an ongoing, bloody and destabilizing civil war, and at worst the occasion for genocidal slaughter like that which occurred in Bosnia four years earlier?

1.3 The Bosnian case – in particular the failure by the United Nations and others to prevent the massacre of thousands of civilians seeking shelter in UN "safe areas" in Srebrenica in 1995 – is another which has had a major impact on the contemporary policy debate about intervention for human protection purposes. It raises the principle that intervention amounts to a promise to people in need: a promise cruelly betrayed. Yet another was the failure and ultimate withdrawal of the UN peace operations in Somalia in 1992–93, when an international intervention to save lives and restore order was destroyed by flawed planning, poor execution, and an excessive dependence on military force.

1.4 These four cases occurred at a time when there were heightened expectations for effective collective action following the end of the Cold War. All four of them – Rwanda, Kosovo, Bosnia and Somalia – have had a profound effect on how the problem of intervention is viewed, analyzed and characterized.

1.5 The basic lines in the contemporary policy debate, one constantly being re-engaged at UN headquarters in New York and in capitals around the world, have been clearly enough drawn. For some, the international community is not intervening enough; for others it is intervening much too often. For some, the only real issue is in ensuring that coercive interventions are effective; for others, questions about legality, process and the possible misuse of precedent loom much larger. For some, the new interventions herald a new world in which human rights trumps state sovereignty; for others, it ushers in a world in which big powers ride roughshod over the smaller ones, manipulating the rhetoric of humanitarianism and human rights. The controversy has laid bare basic divisions within the international community. In the interest of all those victims who suffer and die when leadership and institutions fail, it is crucial that these divisions be resolved.

1.6   In an address to the 54th session of the UN General Assembly in September 1999, Secretary-General Kofi Annan reflected upon "the prospects for human security and inter-vention in the next century." He recalled the failures of the Security Council to act in Rwanda and Kosovo, and challenged the member states of the UN to "find common ground in upholding the principles of the Charter, and acting in defence of our common humanity." The Secretary-General warned that "If the collective conscience of humanity ... cannot find in the United Nations its greatest tribune, there is a grave danger that it will look elsewhere for peace and for justice." In his Millennium Report to the General Assembly a year later, he restated the dilemma, and repeated the challenge:

> ... if humanitarian intervention is, indeed, an unacceptable assault on sovereignty, how should we respond to a Rwanda, to a Srebrenica – to gross and systematic violations of human rights that offend every precept of our common humanity?

1.7   In September 2000, the Government of Canada responded to the Secretary-General's challenge by announcing the establishment of this independent International Commission on Intervention and State Sovereignty (ICISS). Our mandate was generally to build a broader understanding of the problem of reconciling intervention for human protection purposes and sovereignty; more specifically, it was to try to develop a global political consensus on how to move from polemics – and often paralysis – towards action within the international system, particularly through the United Nations. The membership of the Commission was intended to fairly reflect developed and developing country perspectives, and to ensure that we represented between us a wide range of geographical backgrounds, viewpoints, and experiences – with opinions, at least at the outset, reflecting the main lines of the current international debate. If we could produce consensus among ourselves, there was at least a chance that we might be able to encourage it in the wider international community.

1.8   The Commission met for the first time on 5–6 November 2000, in Ottawa. A year-long strategy for carrying out our mandate was there mapped out, with agreement that our work process should be transparent, inclusive, and global. The Government of Canada supported the establishment of a research directorate, and with assistance from a number of other governments and major foundations, sponsored and organized a series of regional roundtables and national consultations intended to expose the Commission to a wide and diverse range of views, while at the same time helping to inform public opinion about our work and objectives. Particular emphasis was placed on the need to ensure that views of affected populations were heard and taken into account, in addition to the views of governments, intergovernmental and non-governmental organizations (NGOs), and civil society representatives.

1.9   The Commission was strongly committed from the outset to consulting as widely as possible around the world, including in the countries of all five permanent members of the Security Council. Over the course of a year, accordingly, roundtable meetings or consultations were conducted in Beijing, Cairo, Geneva, London, Maputo, New Delhi, New York, Ottawa, Paris, St Petersburg, Santiago and Washington. The discussions at those meetings were invariably rich and rewarding; they are summarized in the supplementary volume accompanying this report. In addition, individual Commissioners and members of the research team attended a large number of conferences and seminars – often by special invitation or in a representative capacity. The Commission has also made a particular effort to consult a broad range of academic thinking and expertise; much of this analysis and advice is embodied in the research papers and bibliography contained in the supplementary volume.

THE CHANGING INTERNATIONAL ENVIRONMENT

1.10   The issues and preoccupations of the 21st century present new and often fundamentally different types of challenges from those that faced the world in 1945, when the United Nations was founded. As new realities and challenges have emerged, so too have new expectations for action and new standards of conduct in national and international affairs. Since, for example, the terrorist attacks of 11 September 2001 on the World Trade Center and Pentagon, it has become evident that the war against terrorism the world must now fight – one with no contested frontiers and a largely invisible enemy – is one like no other war before it.

1.11 Many new international institutions have been created to meet these changed circumstances. In key respects, however, the mandates and capacity of international institutions have not kept pace with international needs or modern expectations. Above all, the issue of international intervention for human protection purposes is a clear and compelling example of concerted action urgently being needed to bring international norms and institutions in line with international needs and expectations.

1.12   The current debate on intervention for human protection purposes is itself both a product and a reflection of how much has changed since the UN was established. The current debate takes place in the context of a broadly expanded range of state, non-state, and institutional actors, and increasingly evident interaction and interdependence among them. It is a debate that reflects new sets of issues and new types of concerns. It is a debate that is being conducted within the framework of new standards of conduct for states and individuals, and in a context of greatly increased expectations for action. And it is a debate that takes place within an institutional framework that since the end of the Cold War has held out the prospect of effective joint international action to address issues of peace, security, human rights and sustainable development on a global scale.

New Actors

1.13   With new actors – not least new states, with the UN growing from 51 member states in 1945 to 189 today – has come a wide range of new voices, perspectives, interests, experiences and aspirations. Together, these new international actors have added both depth and texture to the increasingly rich tapestry of international society and important institutional credibility and practical expertise to the wider debate.

1.14   Prominent among the range of important new actors are a number of institutional actors and mechanisms, especially in the areas of human rights and human security. They have included, among others, the UN High Commissioner for Human Rights and the

International Criminal Tribunal for the former Yugoslavia, both created in 1993, and its sister tribunals for Rwanda established in 1994 and Sierra Leone in 2001. The International Criminal Court, whose creation was decided in 1998, will begin operation when 60 countries have ratified its Statute. In addition to the new institutions, established ones such as the UN High Commissioner for Refugees, and the ICRC and International Federation of Red Cross and Red Crescent Societies, have been ever more active.

1.15   Nearly as significant has been the emergence, of many new non-state actors in international affairs – including especially a large number of NGOs dealing with global matters; a growing number of media and academic institutions with worldwide reach; and an increasingly diverse array of armed non-state actors ranging from national and international terrorists to traditional rebel movements and various organized criminal groupings. These new non-state actors, good or bad, have forced the debate about intervention for human protection purposes to be conducted in front of a broader public, while at the same time adding new elements to the agenda.

New Security Issues

1.16   The current debate about intervention for human protection purposes takes place in a context not just of new actors, but also of new sets of issues. The most marked security phenomenon since the end of the Cold War has been the proliferation of armed conflict within states. In most cases these conflicts have centred on demands for greater political rights and other political objectives, demands that were in many cases forcibly suppressed during the Cold War. Gone with the end of the Cold War was the artificial and often very brutal check which Cold War politics imposed on the political development of many states and societies – especially in the developing world and in the former Eastern Bloc. In many states, the result of the end of the Cold War has been a new emphasis on democratization, human rights and good governance. But in too many others, the result has been internal war or civil conflict – more often than not with ugly political and humanitarian repercussions.

1.17   In other cases, conflict has been directed towards the capture of resources and towards plunder. The weakness of state structures and institutions in many countries has heightened the challenges and risks of nation building, and sometimes tempted armed groups to try to seize and themselves exploit valuable assets such as diamonds, timber and other natural resources, not to mention the raw materials of drug production.

1.18   These internal conflicts are made more complex and lethal by modern technology and communications, and in particular by the proliferation of cheap, highly destructive weapons which find their way into the hands, among others, of child soldiers. Many occur in desperately poor societies, or societies where there is a single valuable commodity – like oil or diamonds – which rapidly becomes the fuel which sustains a full-time war economy. In these places, the state's monopoly over the means of violence is lost, and violence becomes a way of life with catastrophic consequences for civilians caught in the crossfire.

1.19   An unhappy trend of contemporary conflict has been the increased vulnerability of civilians, often involving their deliberate targeting. Sometimes the permanent displacement of civilian populations has been a primary objective of the conflict; there has also been increasing concern about the deliberate use of systematic rape to provoke exclusion from a group. Efforts to suppress armed (and sometimes unarmed) dissent have in too many cases led to excessive and disproportionate actions by governments, producing in some cases excessive and unwarranted suffering on the part of civilian populations. In a few cases, regimes have launched campaigns of terror on their own populations, sometimes in the name of an ideology; sometimes spurred on by racial, religious or ethnic hatred; and sometimes purely for personal gain or plunder. In other cases they have supported or abetted terror campaigns aimed at other countries which have resulted in major destruction and loss of life.

1.20   Intra-state warfare is often viewed, in the prosperous West, simply as a set of discrete and unrelated crises occurring in distant and unimportant regions. In reality, what is happening is a convulsive process of state fragmentation and state formation that is transforming the international order itself. Moreover, the rich world is deeply implicated in the process. Civil conflicts are fuelled by arms and monetary transfers that originate in the developed world, and their destabilizing effects are felt in the developed world in everything from globally interconnected terrorism to refugee flows, the export of drugs, the spread of infectious disease and organized crime.

1.21   These considerations reinforce the Commission's view that human security is indeed indivisible. There is no longer such a thing as a humanitarian catastrophe occurring "in a faraway country of which we know little." On 11 September 2001 global terrorism, with its roots in complex conflicts in distant lands, struck the US homeland: impregnable lines of continental defence proved an illusion even for the world's most powerful state. At the same time, around 40 per cent of the victims of the World Trade Center attacks were non-Americans, from some 80 countries. In an interdependent world, in which security depends on a framework of stable sovereign entities, the existence of fragile states, failing states, states who through weakness or ill-will harbour those dangerous to others, or states that can only maintain internal order by means of gross human rights violations, can constitute a risk to people everywhere.

1.22   All this presents the international community with acute dilemmas. If it stays disengaged, there is the risk of becoming complicit bystanders in massacre, ethnic cleansing, and even genocide. If the international community intervenes, it may or may not be able to mitigate such abuses. But even when it does, intervention sometimes means taking sides in intra-state conflicts. Once it does so, the international community may only be aiding in the further fragmentation of the state system. Interventions in the Balkans did manage to reduce the civilian death toll, but it has yet to produce a stable state order in the region. As both the Kosovo and Bosnian interventions show, even when the goal of international action is, as it should be, protecting ordinary human beings from gross and systematic abuse, it can be difficult to avoid doing rather more harm than good.

1.23   Building a stable order after intervention for human protection purposes remains an equally great challenge. Finding a consensus about intervention is not simply a matter of deciding who should authorize it and when it is legitimate to undertake. It is also a matter of figuring out how to do it so that decent objectives are not tarnished by inappropriate means. As is widely recognized, UN peacekeeping strategies, crafted for an era of war between states and designed to monitor and reinforce ceasefires agreed between belligerents, may no longer be suitable to protect civilians caught in the middle of bloody struggles between states and insurgents. The challenge in this context is to find tactics and strategies of military intervention that fill the current gulf between outdated concepts of peacekeeping and full-scale military operations that may have deleterious impacts on civilians.

1.24   There is a further challenge: crafting responses that are consistent. Thanks to modern media, some humanitarian crises receive a surfeit of attention, while others languish in indifference and neglect. Some crises are exaggerated by media coverage and ill-considered calls for action skew the response of the international community in an inconsistent and undisciplined manner. Yet perfect consistency is not always possible: the sheer number of crises with serious humanitarian dimensions precludes an effective response in each case. Moreover, there are some cases where international action is precluded by the opposition of a Permanent Five member or other major power. But can the fact that effective international action is not always possible in every instance of major humanitarian catastrophe ever be an excuse for inaction where effective responses are possible?

New Demands and Expectations

1.25   The current debate about intervention for human protection purposes also takes place in a historical, political and legal context of evolving international standards of conduct for states and individuals, including the development of new and stronger norms and mechanisms for the protection of human rights. Human rights have now become a mainstream part of international law, and respect for human rights a central subject and responsibility of international relations. Some key milestones in this progression have been the Universal Declaration of Human Rights; the four Geneva Conventions and the two Additional Protocols on international humanitarian law in armed conflict; the 1948 Convention on the Prevention and Punishment of the Crime of Genocide; the two 1966 Covenants relating to civil, political, social, economic and cultural rights; and the adoption in 1998 of the statute for the establishment of an International Criminal Court. Even though in some cases imperfectly implemented, these agreements and mechanisms have significantly changed expectations at all levels about what is and what is not acceptable conduct by states and other actors.

1.26   The universal jurisdiction established in the Geneva Conventions and Additional Protocols (as well as the Convention Against Torture) means any state party in which a person accused of the crimes listed in them is found can bring that person to trial. Universal jurisdiction is also available under customary international law, and associated state legislation, for genocide and crimes against humanity. The recent Pinochet case in the UK and the conviction in Belgium for complicity in genocide of Rwandan nuns are an indication that the universal jurisdiction of these instruments is starting to be taken very seriously.

1.27   The change in law and in legal norms has been accompanied by the establishment, as has been noted, of a broad range of new international institutions and non-governmental organizations, concerned to monitor and promote the implementation worldwide of human rights and international humanitarian law – with the result that new expectations for conduct are increasingly accompanied by new expectations for corrective action.

1.28   The concept of human security – including concern for human rights, but broader than that in its scope – has also become an increasingly important element in international law and international relations, increasingly providing a conceptual framework for international action. Although the issue is far from uncontroversial, the concept of security is now increasingly recognized to extend to people as well as to states. It is certainly becoming increasingly clear that the human impact of international actions cannot be regarded as collateral to other actions, but must be a central preoccupation for all concerned. Whether universally popular or not, there is growing recognition worldwide that the protection of human security, including human rights and human dignity, must be one of the fundamental objectives of modern international institutions.

1.29   In considering changing expectations and conduct, nationally and internationally, it is impossible to ignore here the impact of globalization and technology. The revolution in information technology has made global communications instantaneous and provided unprecedented access to information worldwide. The result has been an enormously

heightened awareness of conflicts wherever they may be occurring, combined with immediate and often very compelling visual images of the resultant suffering on television and in
other mass media. In September 2001 the world suffered and grieved with Americans.
Equally, killing and conflict occurring not only in major capitals but in distant places
around the world has been brought right into the homes and living rooms of people all over
the world. In a number of cases, popular concern over what has been seen has put political
pressure on governments to respond. For many of these governments, it has created a
domestic political cost for inaction and indifference.

New Opportunities for Common Action

1.30   A critically important contextual dimension of the current debate on intervention for
human protection purposes is the new opportunity and capacity for common action that
have resulted from the end of the Cold War. For perhaps the first time since the UN was established, there is now a genuine prospect of the Security Council fulfilling the role envisioned
for it in the UN Charter. Despite some notable setbacks, the capacity for common action by
the Security Council was shown during the 1990s to be real, with the authorization by the
Council of nearly 40 peacekeeping or peace enforcement operations over the last decade.

1.31   Closely allied to this new awareness of world conditions and new visibility for human
suffering has been the impact of globalization in intensifying economic interdependence
between states. Globalization has led to closer ties at all levels and a pronounced trend
towards multilateral cooperation. In the context of the debate surrounding the issue of
intervention for human protection purposes, it is clear that the realities of globalization and
growing interdependency have often been important factors in prompting neighbouring
states and others to become engaged positively both in promoting prevention, and also in
calling for intervention in situations that seem to be spiralling out of control.

THE IMPLICATIONS FOR STATE SOVEREIGNTY

1.32   In a dangerous world marked by overwhelming inequalities of power and resources,
sovereignty is for many states their best – and sometimes seemingly their only – line of
defence. But sovereignty is more than just a functional principle of international relations.
For many states and peoples, it is also a recognition of their equal worth and dignity, a
protection of their unique identities and their national freedom, and an affirmation of their
right to shape and determine their own destiny. In recognition of this, the principle that all
states are equally sovereign under international law was established as a cornerstone of the
UN Charter (Article 2.1).

1.33   However, for all the reasons mentioned already, the conditions under which sovereignty is exercised – and intervention is practised – have changed dramatically since 1945.
Many new states have emerged and are still in the process of consolidating their identity.
Evolving international law has set many constraints on what states can do, and not only in
the realm of human rights. The emerging concept of human security has created additional
demands and expectations in relation to the way states treat their own people. And many new
actors are playing international roles previously more or less the exclusive preserve of states.

1.34   All that said, sovereignty does still matter. It is strongly arguable that effective and
legitimate states remain the best way to ensure that the benefits of the internationalization
of trade, investment, technology and communication will be equitably shared. Those states
which can call upon strong regional alliances, internal peace, and a strong and independent
civil society, seem clearly best placed to benefit from globalization. They will also be likely

to be those most respectful of human rights. And in security terms, a cohesive and peaceful international system is far more likely to be achieved through the cooperation of effective states, confident of their place in the world, than in an environment of fragile, collapsed, fragmenting or generally chaotic state entities.

1.35   The defence of state sovereignty, by even its strongest supporters, does not include any claim of the unlimited power of a state to do what it wants to its own people. The Commission heard no such claim at any stage during our worldwide consultations. It is acknowledged that sovereignty implies a dual responsibility: externally – to respect the sovereignty of other states, and internally, to respect the dignity and basic rights of all the people within the state. In international human rights covenants, in UN practice, and in state practice itself, sovereignty is now understood as embracing this dual responsibility. Sovereignty as responsibility has become the minimum content of good international citizenship.

1.36   This modern understanding of the meaning of sovereignty is of central importance in the Commission's approach to the question of intervention for human protection purposes, and in particular in the development of our core theme, "the responsibility to protect," which is introduced and explained in the next chapter.

THE MEANING OF INTERVENTION

Scope of the Concept

1.37   Part of the controversy over "intervention" derives from the potential width of activities this term can cover, up to and including military intervention. Some would regard any application of pressure to a state as being intervention, and would include in this conditional support programmes by major international financial institutions whose recipients often feel they have no choice but to accept. Some others would regard almost any non-consensual interference in the internal affairs of another state as being intervention – including the delivery of emergency relief assistance to a section of a country's population in need. Others again would regard any kind of outright coercive actions – not just military action but actual or threatened political and economic sanctions, blockades, diplomatic and military threats, and international criminal prosecutions – as all being included in the term. Yet others would confine its use to military force.

1.38   The kind of intervention with which we are concerned in this report is action taken against a state or its leaders, without its or their consent, for purposes which are claimed to be humanitarian or protective. By far the most controversial form of such intervention is military, and a great part of our report necessarily focuses on that. But we are also very much concerned with alternatives to military action, including all forms of preventive measures, and coercive intervention measures – sanctions and criminal prosecutions – falling short of military intervention. Such coercive measures are discussed in this report in two contexts: their threatened use as a preventive measure, designed to avoid the need for military intervention arising (Chapter 3); and their actual use as a reactive measure, but as an alternative to military force (Chapter 4).

"Humanitarian" Intervention?

1.39   The Commission recognizes the long history, and continuing wide and popular usage, of the phrase "humanitarian intervention," and also its descriptive usefulness in clearly focusing attention on one particular category of interventions – namely, those undertaken for the stated purpose of protecting or assisting people at risk. But we have made a deliberate decision not to adopt this terminology, preferring to refer either to "intervention," or as appropriate "military intervention," for human protection purposes.

1.40   We have responded in this respect to the very strong opposition expressed by human-itarian agencies, humanitarian organizations and humanitarian workers towards any militar-ization of the word "humanitarian": whatever the motives of those engaging in the inter-vention, it is anathema for the humanitarian relief and assistance sector to have this word appropriated to describe any kind of military action. The Commission has also been respons-ive to the suggestion in some political quarters that use in this context of an inherently approving word like "humanitarian" tends to prejudge the very question in issue – that is, whether the intervention is in fact defensible.

1.41   We have taken the view from the outset that there is some virtue in anything which may encourage people to look again, with fresh eyes, at the real issues involved in the sovereignty–intervention debate. Beyond the question of "humanitarian intervention" terminology, there is a rather larger language change, and associated reconceptualization of the issues, which the Commission has also felt it helpful to embrace. It is to this – the concept of "the responsibility to protect" – that we turn in the next chapter.

2. A NEW APPROACH: "THE RESPONSIBILITY TO PROTECT"

2.1   Millions of human beings remain at the mercy of civil wars, insurgencies, state repression and state collapse. This is a stark and undeniable reality, and it is at the heart of all the issues with which this Commission has been wrestling. What is at stake here is not making the world safe for big powers, or trampling over the sovereign rights of small ones, but delivering practical protection for ordinary people, at risk of their lives, because their states are unwilling or unable to protect them.

2.2   But all this is easier said than done. There have been as many failures as successes, perhaps more, in the international protective record in recent years. There are continuing fears about a "right to intervene" being formally acknowledged. If intervention for human protection purposes is to be accepted, including the possibility of military action, it remains imperative that the international community develop consistent, credible and enforceable standards to guide state and intergovernmental practice. The experience and aftermath of Somalia, Rwanda, Srebrenica and Kosovo, as well as interventions and non-interventions in a number of other places, have provided a clear indication that the tools, devices and thinking of international relations need now to be comprehensively reassessed, in order to meet the foreseeable needs of the 21st century.

2.3   Any new approach to intervention on human protection grounds needs to meet at least four basic objectives:

❑ to establish clearer rules, procedures and criteria for determining whether, when and how to intervene;

❑ to establish the legitimacy of military intervention when necessary and after all other approaches have failed;

❑ to ensure that military intervention, when it occurs, is carried out only for the purposes proposed, is effective, and is undertaken with proper concern to minimize the human costs and institutional damage that will result; and

❑ to help eliminate, where possible, the causes of conflict while enhancing the prospects for durable and sustainable peace.

2.4   In the later chapters of this report we spell out in detail how these objectives might be met. But there is a significant preliminary issue which must first be addressed. It is important that language – and the concepts which lie behind particular choices of words – do not become a barrier to dealing with the real issues involved. Just as the Commission found that the expression "humanitarian intervention" did not help to carry the debate forward, so too do we believe that the language of past debates arguing for or against a "right to intervene" by one state on the territory of another state is outdated and unhelpful. We prefer to talk not of a "right to intervene" but of a "responsibility to protect."

2.5   Changing the language of the debate, while it can remove a barrier to effective action, does not, of course, change the substantive issues which have to be addressed. There still remain to be argued all the moral, legal, political and operational questions – about need, authority, will and capacity respectively – which have themselves been so difficult and divisive. But if people are prepared to look at all these issues from the new perspective that we propose, it may just make finding agreed answers that much easier.

2.6   In the remainder of this chapter we seek to make a principled, as well as a practical and political, case for conceptualizing the intervention issue in terms of a responsibility to protect. The building blocks of the argument are first, the principles inherent in the concept of sovereignty; and secondly, the impact of emerging principles of human rights and human security, and changing state and intergovernmental practice.

THE MEANING OF SOVEREIGNTY

The Norm of Non-Intervention

2.7   Sovereignty has come to signify, in the Westphalian concept, the legal identity of a state in international law. It is a concept which provides order, stability and predictability in international relations since sovereign states are regarded as equal, regardless of comparative size or wealth. The principle of sovereign equality of states is enshrined in Article 2.1 of the UN Charter. Internally, sovereignty signifies the capacity to make authoritative decisions with regard to the people and resources within the territory of the state. Generally, however, the authority of the state is not regarded as absolute, but constrained and regulated internally by constitutional power sharing arrangements.

2.8   A condition of any one state's sovereignty is a corresponding obligation to respect every other state's sovereignty: the norm of non-intervention is enshrined in Article 2.7 of the UN Charter. A sovereign state is empowered in international law to exercise exclusive and total jurisdiction within its territorial borders. Other states have the corresponding duty not to intervene in the internal affairs of a sovereign state. If that duty is violated, the victim state has the further right to defend its territorial integrity and political independence. In the era of decolonization, the sovereign equality of states and the correlative norm of non-intervention received its most emphatic affirmation from the newly independent states.

2.9   At the same time, while intervention for human protection purposes was extremely rare, during the Cold War years state practice reflected the unwillingness of many countries to give up the use of intervention for political or other purposes as an instrument of policy. Leaders on both sides of the ideological divide intervened in support of friendly leaders against local populations, while also supporting rebel movements and other opposition causes in states to which they were ideologically opposed. None were prepared to rule out *a priori* the use of force in another country in order to rescue nationals who were trapped and threatened there.

2.10   The established and universally acknowledged right to self-defence, embodied in Article 51 of the UN Charter, was sometimes extended to include the right to launch punitive raids into neighbouring countries that had shown themselves unwilling or unable to stop their territory from being used as a launching pad for cross-border armed raids or terrorist attacks. But all that said, the many examples of intervention in actual state practice through-out the 20th century did not lead to an abandonment of the norm of non-intervention.

The Organizing Principle of the UN System

2.11   Membership of the United Nations was the final symbol of independent sovereign statehood and thus the seal of acceptance into the community of nations. The UN also became the principal international forum for collaborative action in the shared pursuit of the three goals of state building, nation building and economic development. The UN was therefore the main arena for the jealous protection, not the casual abrogation, of state sovereignty.

2.12   The UN is an organization dedicated to the maintenance of international peace and security on the basis of protecting the territorial integrity, political independence and national sovereignty of its member states. But the overwhelming majority of today's armed conflicts are internal, not inter-state. Moreover, the proportion of civilians killed in them increased from about one in ten at the start of the 20th century to around nine in ten by its close. This has presented the organization with a major difficulty: how to reconcile its foundational principles of member states' sovereignty and the accompanying primary mandate to maintain international peace and security ("to save succeeding generations from the scourge of war") – with the equally compelling mission to promote the interests and welfare of people within those states ("We the peoples of the United Nations").

2.13   The Secretary-General has discussed the dilemma in the conceptual language of two notions of sovereignty, one vesting in the state, the second in the people and in individuals. His approach reflects the ever-increasing commitment around the world to democratic government (of, by and for the people) and greater popular freedoms. The second notion of sovereignty to which he refers should not be seen as any kind of challenge to the traditional notion of state sovereignty. Rather it is a way of saying that the more traditional notion of state sovereignty should be able comfortably to embrace the goal of greater self-empowerment and freedom for people, both individually and collectively.

Sovereignty as Responsibility

2.14   The Charter of the UN is itself an example of an international obligation voluntarily accepted by member states. On the one hand, in granting membership of the UN, the international community welcomes the signatory state as a responsible member of the community of nations. On the other hand, the state itself, in signing the Charter, accepts the responsibilities of membership flowing from that signature. There is no transfer or dilution of state sovereignty. But there is a necessary re-characterization involved: from *sovereignty as control* to *sovereignty as responsibility* in both internal functions and external duties.

2.15   Thinking of sovereignty as responsibility, in a way that is being increasingly recognized in state practice, has a threefold significance. First, it implies that the state authorities are responsible for the functions of protecting the safety and lives of citizens and promotion of their welfare. Secondly, it suggests that the national political authorities are responsible to the citizens internally and to the international community through the UN. And thirdly, it means that the agents of state are responsible for their actions; that is to say, they are accountable for their acts of commission and omission. The case for thinking of sovereignty in these terms is strengthened by the ever-increasing impact of international human rights norms, and the increasing impact in international discourse of the concept of human security.

HUMAN RIGHTS, HUMAN SECURITY AND EMERGING PRACTICE

Human Rights

2.16   The adoption of new standards of conduct for states in the protection and advancement of international human rights has been one of the great achievements of the post-World
War II era. Article 1.3 of its founding 1945 Charter committed the UN to "promoting and
encouraging respect for human rights and for fundamental freedoms for all without distinction as to race, sex, language or religion." The Universal Declaration of Human Rights (1948)
embodies the moral code, political consensus and legal synthesis of human rights. The
simplicity of the Declaration's language belies the passion of conviction underpinning it. Its
elegance has been the font of inspiration down the decades; its provisions comprise
the vocabulary of complaint. The two Covenants of 1966, on civil–political and social–
economic–cultural rights, affirm and proclaim the human rights norm as a fundamental
principle of international relations and add force and specificity to the Universal Declaration.

2.17   Together the Universal Declaration and the two Covenants mapped out the international human rights agenda, established the benchmark for state conduct, inspired provisions in many national laws and international conventions, and led to the creation of
long-term national infrastructures for the protection and promotion of human rights. They
are important milestones in the transition from a culture of violence to a more enlightened
culture of peace.

2.18   What has been gradually emerging is a parallel transition from a culture of sovereign
impunity to a culture of national and international accountability. International organizations, civil society activists and NGOs use the international human rights norms and instruments as the concrete point of reference against which to judge state conduct. Between
them, the UN and NGOs have achieved many successes. National laws and international
instruments have been improved, a number of political prisoners have been freed and some
victims of abuse have been compensated. The most recent advances in international human
rights have been in the further development of international humanitarian law, for example
in the Ottawa Convention on landmines which subordinated military calculations to
humanitarian concerns about a weapon that cannot distinguish a soldier from a child, and
in the Rome Statute establishing the International Criminal Court.

2.19   Just as the substance of human rights law is coming increasingly closer to realizing the
notion of universal justice – justice without borders – so too is the process. Not only have
new international criminal tribunals been specially created to deal with crimes against
humanity committed in the Balkans, Rwanda and Sierra Leone; and not only is an
International Criminal Court about to be established to try such crimes wherever and whenever committed in the future; but, as already noted in Chapter 1, the universal jurisdiction
which now exists under a number of treaties, like the Geneva Conventions, and which
enables any state party to try anyone accused of the crimes in question, is now beginning to
be seriously applied.

2.20   The significance of these developments in establishing new standards of behaviour,
and new means of enforcing those standards, is unquestionable. But the key to the effective
observance of human rights remains, as it always has been, national law and practice: the
frontline defence of the rule of law is best conducted by the judicial systems of sovereign
states, which should be independent, professional and properly resourced. It is only when
national systems of justice either cannot or will not act to judge crimes against humanity
that universal jurisdiction and other international options should come into play.

Human Security

2.21   The meaning and scope of security have become much broader since the UN Charter was signed in 1945. Human security means the security of people – their physical safety, their economic and social well-being, respect for their dignity and worth as human beings, and the protection of their human rights and fundamental freedoms. The growing recognition world-wide that concepts of security must include people as well as states has marked an important shift in international thinking during the past decade. Secretary-General Kofi Annan himself put the issue of human security at the centre of the current debate, when in his statement to the 54th session of the General Assembly he made clear his intention to "address the prospects for human security and intervention in the next century."

2.22   This Commission certainly accepts that issues of sovereignty and intervention are not just matters affecting the rights or prerogatives of states, but that they deeply affect and involve individual human beings in fundamental ways. One of the virtues of expressing the key issue in this debate as "the responsibility to protect" is that it focuses attention where it should be most concentrated, on the human needs of those seeking protection or assistance. The emphasis in the security debate shifts, with this focus, from territorial security, and security through armaments, to security through human development with access to food and employment, and to environmental security. The fundamental components of human security – the security of *people* against threats to life, health, livelihood, personal safety and human dignity – can be put at risk by external aggression, but also by factors within a country, including "security" forces. Being wedded still to too narrow a concept of "national security" may be one reason why many governments spend more to protect their citizens against undefined external military attack than to guard them against the omnipresent enemies of good health and other real threats to human security on a daily basis.

2.23   The traditional, narrow perception of security leaves out the most elementary and legitimate concerns of ordinary people regarding security in their daily lives. It also diverts enormous amounts of national wealth and human resources into armaments and armed forces, while countries fail to protect their citizens from chronic insecurities of hunger, disease, inadequate shelter, crime, unemployment, social conflict and environmental hazard. When rape is used as an instrument of war and ethnic cleansing, when thousands are killed by floods resulting from a ravaged countryside and when citizens are killed by their own security forces, then it is just insufficient to think of security in terms of national or territorial security alone. The concept of human security can and does embrace such diverse circumstances.

Emerging Practice

2.24   The debate on military intervention for human protection purposes was ignited in the international community essentially because of the critical gap between, on the one hand, the needs and distress being felt, and seen to be felt, in the real world, and on the other hand the codified instruments and modalities for managing world order. There has been a parallel gap, no less critical, between the codified best practice of international behaviour as articulated in the UN Charter and actual state practice as it has evolved in the 56 years since the Charter was signed. While there is not yet a sufficiently strong basis to claim the emergence of a new principle of customary international law, growing state and regional organization practice as well as Security Council precedent suggest an emerging guiding principle – which in the Commission's view could properly be termed "the responsibility to protect."

2.25 The emerging principle in question is that intervention for human protection purposes, including military intervention in extreme cases, is supportable when major harm to civilians is occurring or imminently apprehended, and the state in question is unable or unwilling to end the harm, or is itself the perpetrator. The Security Council itself has been increasingly prepared in recent years to act on this basis, most obviously in Somalia, defining what was essentially an internal situation as constituting a threat to international peace and security such as to justify enforcement action under Chapter VII of the UN Charter. This is also the basis on which the interventions by the Economic Community of West African States (ECOWAS) in Liberia and Sierra Leone were essentially justified by the interveners, as was the intervention mounted without Security Council authorization by NATO allies in Kosovo.

2.26 The notion that there is an emerging guiding principle in favour of military intervention for human protection purposes is also supported by a wide variety of legal sources – including sources that exist independently of any duties, responsibilities or authority that may be derived from Chapter VII of the UN Charter. These legal foundations include fundamental natural law principles; the human rights provisions of the UN Charter; the Universal Declaration of Human Rights together with the Genocide Convention; the Geneva Conventions and Additional Protocols on international humanitarian law; the statute of the International Criminal Court; and a number of other international human rights and human protection agreements and covenants. Some of the ramifications and consequences of these developments will be addressed again in Chapter 6 of this report as part of the examination of the question of authority.

2.27 Based on our reading of state practice, Security Council precedent, established norms, emerging guiding principles, and evolving customary international law, the Commission believes that the Charter's strong bias against military intervention is not to be regarded as absolute when decisive action is required on human protection grounds. The degree of legitimacy accorded to intervention will usually turn on the answers to such questions as the purpose, the means, the exhaustion of other avenues of redress against grievances, the proportionality of the riposte to the initiating provocation, and the agency of authorization. These are all questions that will recur: for present purposes the point is simply that there is a large and accumulating body of law and practice which supports the notion that, whatever form the exercise of that responsibility may properly take, members of the broad community of states do have a responsibility to protect both their own citizens and those of other states as well.

SHIFTING THE TERMS OF THE DEBATE

2.28 The traditional language of the sovereignty–intervention debate – in terms of "the right of humanitarian intervention" or the "right to intervene" – is unhelpful in at least three key respects. First, it necessarily focuses attention on the claims, rights and prerogatives of the potentially intervening states much more so than on the urgent needs of the potential beneficiaries of the action. Secondly, by focusing narrowly on the act of intervention, the traditional language does not adequately take into account the need for either prior preventive effort or subsequent follow-up assistance, both of which have been too often neglected in practice. And thirdly, although this point should not be overstated, the familiar language does effectively operate to trump sovereignty with intervention at the outset of the debate: it loads the dice in favour of intervention before the argument has even begun, by tending to label and delegitimize dissent as anti-humanitarian.

2.29 The Commission is of the view that the debate about intervention for human protection purposes should focus not on "the right to intervene" but on "the responsibility to protect." The proposed change in terminology is also a change in perspective, reversing the perceptions inherent in the traditional language, and adding some additional ones:

❑ First, the responsibility to protect implies an evaluation of the issues from the point of view of those seeking or needing support, rather than those who may be considering intervention. Our preferred terminology refocuses the international searchlight back where it should always be: on the duty to protect communities from mass killing, women from systematic rape and children from starvation.

❑ Secondly, the responsibility to protect acknowledges that the primary responsibility in this regard rests with the state concerned, and that it is only if the state is unable or unwilling to fulfill this responsibility, or is itself the perpetrator, that it becomes the responsibility of the international community to act in its place. In many cases, the state will seek to acquit its responsibility in full and active partnership with representatives of the international community. Thus the "responsibility to protect" is more of a linking concept that bridges the divide between intervention and sovereignty; the language of the "right or duty to intervene" is intrinsically more confrontational.

❑ Thirdly, the responsibility to protect means not just the "responsibility to react," but the "responsibility to prevent" and the "responsibility to rebuild" as well. It directs our attention to the costs and results of action versus no action, and provides conceptual, normative and operational linkages between assistance, intervention and reconstruction.

2.30   The Commission believes that responsibility to protect resides first and foremost with the state whose people are directly affected. This fact reflects not only international law and the modern state system, but also the practical realities of who is best placed to make a positive difference. The domestic authority is best placed to take action to prevent problems from turning into potential conflicts. When problems arise the domestic authority is also best placed to understand them and to deal with them. When solutions are needed, it is the citizens of a particular state who have the greatest interest and the largest stake in the success of those solutions, in ensuring that the domestic authorities are fully accountable for their actions or inactions in addressing these problems, and in helping to ensure that past problems are not allowed to recur.

2.31   While the state whose people are directly affected has the default responsibility to protect, a residual responsibility also lies with the broader community of states. This fallback responsibility is activated when a particular state is clearly either unwilling or unable to fulfill its responsibility to protect or is itself the actual perpetrator of crimes or atrocities; or where people living outside a particular state are directly threatened by actions taking place there. This responsibility also requires that in some circumstances action must be taken by the broader community of states to support populations that are in jeopardy or under serious threat.

2.32   The substance of the responsibility to protect is the provision of life-supporting protection and assistance to populations at risk. This responsibility has three integral and essential components: not just the responsibility to *react* to an actual or apprehended human catastrophe, but the responsibility to *prevent* it, and the responsibility to *rebuild* after the event. Each of these will be dealt with in detail in chapters of this report. But it is important to emphasize from the start that action in support of the responsibility to protect necessarily involves and calls for a broad range and wide variety of assistance actions and responses. These actions may include both long and short-term measures to help prevent human security-threatening situations from occurring, intensifying, spreading, or persisting; and rebuilding support to help prevent them from recurring; as well as, at least in extreme cases, military intervention to protect at-risk civilians from harm.

2.33 Changing the terms of the debate from "right to intervene" to "responsibility to protect" helps to shift the focus of discussion where it belongs – on the requirements of those who need or seek assistance. But while this is an important and necessary step, it does not by itself, as we have already acknowledged, resolve the difficult questions relating to the circumstances in which the responsibility to protect should be exercised – questions of legitimacy, authority, operational effectiveness and political will. These issues are fully addressed in subsequent chapters. While the Commission does not purport to try to resolve all of these difficult issues now and forever, our approach will hopefully generate innovative thinking on ways of achieving and sustaining effective and appropriate action.

3. THE RESPONSIBILITY TO PREVENT

A COMMITMENT TO PREVENTION

3.1   This Commission strongly believes that the responsibility to protect implies an accompanying responsibility to prevent. And we think that it is more than high time for the international community to be doing more to close the gap between rhetorical support for prevention and tangible commitment. The need to do much better on prevention, and to exhaust prevention options before rushing to embrace intervention, were constantly recurring themes in our worldwide consultations, and ones which we wholeheartedly endorse.

3.2   Prevention of deadly conflict and other forms of man-made catastrophe is, as with all other aspects of the responsibility to protect, first and foremost the responsibility of sovereign states, and the communities and institutions within them. A firm national commitment to ensuring fair treatment and fair opportunities for all citizens provides a solid basis for conflict prevention. Efforts to ensure accountability and good governance, protect human rights, promote social and economic development and ensure a fair distribution of resources point toward the necessary means.

3.3   But conflict prevention is not merely a national or local affair. The failure of prevention can have wide international consequences and costs. Moreover, for prevention to succeed, strong support from the international community is often needed, and in many cases may be indispensable. Such support may take many forms. It may come in the form of development assistance and other efforts to help address the root cause of potential conflict; or efforts to provide support for local initiatives to advance good governance, human rights, or the rule of law; or good offices missions, mediation efforts and other efforts to promote dialogue or reconciliation. In some cases international support for prevention efforts may take the form of inducements; in others, it may involve a willingness to apply tough and perhaps even punitive measures.

3.4   By showing a commitment to helping local efforts to address both the root causes of problems and their more immediate triggers, broader international efforts gain added credibility – domestically, regionally, and globally. This credibility is especially important when international action must go beyond prevention to reaction, and especially when that reaction necessarily involves coercive measures, and ultimately the use of armed force. The basic point of preventive efforts is of course to reduce, and hopefully eliminate, the need for intervention altogether. But even where they have not succeeded in preventing conflict or catastrophe, they are a necessary precondition for responding effectively to it.

3.5   The UN General Assembly and Security Council in 2000 adopted resolutions recognizing the vital role of all parts of the United Nations system in conflict prevention, and pledging to enhance their effectiveness. The *Report of the Panel on United Nations Peace Operations* made much of the need to avoid such operations by more effective prevention. The important report of the Secretary-General on *Prevention of Armed Conflict* in 2001 was another articulate call for renewed focus on cooperation for prevention, with many far-reaching recommendations, especially in addressing deep-rooted structural problems, which this Commission wholly endorses.

3.6   In response to these and other calls over the years, a promising array of international, regional, and non-governmental mechanisms for conflict prevention focused particularly on intra-state conflict was established or expanded in the 1990s. The Organization of African Unity (OAU), for instance, established in 1993 a Mechanism for Conflict Prevention, Management, and Settlement, with support from external donors. The Organization for Security and Cooperation in Europe (OSCE) has developed a number of innovative internal mechanisms and practices toward preventing conflict in Europe. Also important has been the increasingly significant role played by NGOs, particularly in the context of early warning efforts and helping to galvanize domestic and foreign public opinion in support of prevention measures.

3.7   But UN and other resources devoted to prevention in all its forms remain dwarfed by the resources devoted by intergovernmental organizations, and the states themselves, to preparation for war, to warfighting, to coercive intervention, to humanitarian assistance to the victims of conflict and catastrophe, to post-intervention reconstruction, and to peace-keeping. Very often, those with the means to act prefer to play the odds, sometimes betting that the situation will somehow resolve itself, or that it will simmer without reaching a boil, or that the resulting conflict will prove less dire than predicted, or that conflict if it does break out can be quickly contained. The result, according to the Carnegie Commission on Preventing Deadly Conflict, was that the international community spent approximately $200 billion on conflict management in seven major interventions in the 1990s (Bosnia and Herzegovina, Somalia, Rwanda, Haiti, the Persian Gulf, Cambodia and El Salvador), but could have saved $130 billion through a more effective preventive approach.

3.8   There remains a gap between rhetoric and financial and political support for preven-tion. Not the least of the problems here has been with development assistance. While the international community has become increasingly sophisticated in using development assistance to promote conflict prevention, there has in recent years been a marked declined in the overall level of that assistance worldwide. Debts accumulated during the Cold War continue to place a tremendous repayment burden on many hard-pressed developing country economies, making scarce resources even scarcer, exacerbating income gaps within societies, and depriving many countries of the capacity to apply their own resources to conflict prevention. The trade policies applied by many richer industrialized countries, unfairly disadvantaging or restricting access to markets, together with the terms of trade being experienced by many developing countries, have not made any easier the reduction of that debt burden, or the capacity to meet the social and economic development needs of their populations.

3.9   For the effective prevention of conflict, and the related sources of human misery with which this report is concerned, three essential conditions have to be met. First, there has to be knowledge of the fragility of the situation and the risks associated with it – so called "early warning." Second, there has to be understanding of the policy measures available that are capable of making a difference – the so-called "preventive toolbox." And third, there has to be, as always, the willingness to apply those measures – the issue of "political will." We shall say a little about the first two of these conditions in this chapter, and about the third in Chapter 8. An extensive analysis of the modalities of conflict prevention is not the focus of this Commission: this ground has already been amply covered by many others. But in the context of the responsibility to protect, improving conflict prevention at every level – con-ceptually, strategically and operationally – is urgent and essential. Encouraging more serious and sustained efforts to address the root cause of the problems that put populations at risk, as well as more effective use of direct prevention measures, is a key objective of the Commission's efforts.

EARLY WARNING AND ANALYSIS

3.10   It is possible to exaggerate the extent to which lack of early warning is a serious problem in government and intergovernmental organization these days. More often than not what is lacking is not the basic data, but its analysis and translation into policy prescription, and the will to do something about it. Far too often – and the recent reports on the UN response to Rwanda in 1994 confirm this – lack of early warning is an excuse rather than an explanation, and the problem is not lack of warning but of timely response.

3.11   All that said, there is a need for more official resources to be devoted to early warning and analysis. Preventive action is founded upon and proceeds from accurate prediction, but too often preventive analysis, to the extent that it happens at all, fails to take key factors into account, misses key warning signs (and hence misses opportunities for early action), or misreads the problem (thereby resulting in application of the wrong tools). A number of distinct problems weaken analytic capacities to predict violent conflict: the multiplicity of variables associated with root causes of conflict and the complexities of their interactions; the associated absence of reliable models for predicting conflict; and simply the perennial problem of securing accurate information on which to base analyses and action.

3.12   To date, early warning about deadly conflict has been essentially ad hoc and unstructured. A wide range of players has been involved, including embassies and intelligence agencies, UN peacekeeping forces, relief and development NGOs, national and international human rights groups, the International Committee of the Red Cross (ICRC), faith groups, academics, and the media. Quality is variable, and coordination among groups has been rudimentary or non-existent. UN specialized agencies and development NGOs have the advantage of a grass-roots presence in countries, but often lack the expertise, and human resources, and especially the mandate to provide accurate and reliable early-warning information.

3.13   Dissatisfaction with this situation has prompted the rise of a new type of NGO, one dedicated exclusively to conflict early warning. Organizations such as International Crisis Group (ICG) monitor and report on areas of the world where conflict appears to be emerging, and they are aggressive in alerting governments and the media if they believe preventive action is urgently required. Their work is complemented by the monitoring and reporting capacity of international and national human rights organizations such as Amnesty International (AI), Human Rights Watch (HRW) and the Fédération internationale des ligues des droits de l'homme (FIDH). These organizations, which previously devoted most of their energies to reporting on human rights violations against individuals and groups, have made a conscious effort to expand their work to include early warning about conflicts that could result in massive violations of human rights or even genocide. The impressive growth of such indigenous human rights centres in the post-Cold War period gives this set of actors an increasingly powerful network of information and partnerships. Still, it is taking time for these organizations to learn how better to coordinate among themselves, mobilize constituents globally, work with the media, and move governments.

3.14   UN headquarters is often identified as the logical place to centralize early warning. Efforts have been made for over two decades to improve the world organization's information-gathering and analytical capacities. One of the principal strengths is the special mandate provided to the Secretary-General under Article 99 of the UN Charter to "bring to the attention of the Security Council any matter that in his opinion may threaten the maintenance of international peace and security." The Secretariat possesses, in other words, a formidable capacity to alert the world of impending conflicts, either loudly or discreetly. But efforts to improve the organization's early-warning capacity have so far fallen short, and essential intelligence-gathering and analytical capacity will for the foreseeable future largely continue to depend on non-UN sources.

3.15   The *Report of the Panel on United Nations Peace Operations* is one of many that calls for that clearinghouse role to be played by the UN, noting "the need to have more effective collection and assessment at UN headquarters, including an enhanced conflict early-warning system that can detect and recognize the threat or risk of conflict or genocide." That report also makes very detailed proposals for building an early-warning capacity within the UN Secretariat. The Commission fully supports these proposals.

3.16   Efforts to build a better early-warning system by harnessing pre-existing governmental capacity is an idea worth pursuing, but realism is in order about the extent to which states will be willing to divulge information which may compromise their own intelligence network, as well as the degree to which any such information can be relied upon. In order to enhance the capacity of the Secretary-General to provide more timely and accurate information to the Security Council about conflict prone areas, a special unit should be established that can receive and analyze sensitive information from member states and others, and that would report directly to the Secretary-General. The unit should be staffed by a small number of specialized personnel trained in conflict prevention.

3.17   Greater involvement by regional actors with intimate local knowledge is also crucial. Although emerging conflicts tend to share a number of characteristics, each is also unique in some ways. Regional actors are usually better placed to understand local dynamics, although they also have shortcomings – not least of which is that they are often not disinterested in the outcomes of deadly conflicts. The Commission recommends that increased resources be made available to support regional and sub-regional conflict prevention initiatives, as well as capacity building aimed at improving the effectiveness of regional and sub-regional organizations in peacekeeping, peace enforcement and intervention operations.

ROOT CAUSE PREVENTION EFFORTS

3.18   The Security Council itself – the body charged with the primary responsibility for the maintenance of international peace and security – has stressed the importance of responding to the root causes of conflict and the need to pursue long-term effective preventive strategies. This concern is grounded firmly in the UN Charter, Article 55 of which explicitly recognizes that solutions to international economic, social, health and related problems; international, cultural and educational cooperation; and universal respect for human rights are all essential for "the creation of conditions of stability and well-being which are necessary for peaceful and friendly relations among nations." The Charter thus provides the foundation for a comprehensive and long-term approach to conflict prevention based on an expanded concept of peace and security.

3.19   Though there is no universal agreement over the precise causes of deadly conflict, it is common to differentiate between underlying or "root" and precipitating or "direct" causes of armed conflict. There is a growing and widespread recognition that armed conflicts cannot be understood without reference to such "root" causes as poverty, political repression, and uneven distribution of resources. "Every step taken towards reducing poverty and achieving broad-based economic growth," the Secretary-General has stated in his recent report, "is a step toward conflict prevention." Preventive strategies must therefore work "to promote human rights, to protect minority rights and to institute political arrangements in which all groups are represented." Ignoring these underlying factors amounts to addressing the symptoms rather the causes of deadly conflict.

3.20 Conflict prevention measures, like other forms of assistance, are always best implemented when based on detailed knowledge and understanding, and maximum possible cooperation between helpers and those helped. In analyzing the causes of conflict and applying preventive measures it is important that developed countries be aware of the cultural barriers that may inhibit the interpretation of information coming from other countries and regions, and that they overcome any reluctance to examine closely their own policies for evidence of their potential negative impact on developing countries.

3.21 Root cause prevention has many dimensions. It may mean addressing *political* needs and deficiencies, and this might involve democratic institution and capacity building; constitutional power sharing, power-alternating and redistribution arrangements; confidence building measures between different communities or groups; support for press freedom and the rule of law; the promotion of civil society; and other types of similar initiatives that broadly fit within the human security framework.

3.22 Root cause prevention may also mean tackling *economic* deprivation and the lack of economic opportunities. This might involve development assistance and cooperation to address inequities in the distribution of resources or opportunities; promotion of economic growth and opportunity; better terms of trade and permitting greater access to external markets for developing economies; encouraging necessary economic and structural reform; and technical assistance for strengthening regulatory instruments and institutions.

3.23 Root cause prevention may also mean strengthening *legal* protections and institutions. This might involve supporting efforts to strengthen the rule of law; protecting the integrity and independence of the judiciary; promoting honesty and accountability in law enforcement; enhancing protections for vulnerable groups, especially minorities; and providing support to local institutions and organizations working to advance human rights.

3.24 Root cause prevention may also mean embarking upon needed sectoral reforms to the *military* and other state security services. This might involve enhanced education and training for military forces; reintegration of ex-combatants; strengthening civilian control mechanisms, including budget control; encouraging efforts to ensure that security services are accountable for their actions and operate within the law; and promoting adherence to arms control and disarmament and non-proliferation regimes, including control over the transfer of light weapons and small arms, and the prohibition of landmines.

DIRECT PREVENTION EFFORTS

3.25 The direct prevention "toolbox" has essentially the same compartments – political/ diplomatic, economic, legal and military – as the one for root cause prevention, but different instruments, reflecting the shorter time available in which to make a difference. These instruments in each case may take the form of straightforward assistance, positive inducements or, in more difficult cases, the negative form of threatened "punishments." But the essential and common attribute of all these actions and measures is that they aim – even where the cooperation of the state concerned is reluctant – to make it absolutely unnecessary to employ directly coercive measures against the state concerned.

3.26 *Political and diplomatic* direct prevention measures may include the direct involvement of the UN Secretary-General, as well as fact-finding missions, friends groups, eminent persons commissions, dialogue and mediation through good offices, international appeals, and non-official "second track" dialogue and problem-solving workshops. At the negative end of the scale, political and diplomatic direct prevention might encompass the threat or application of political sanctions, diplomatic isolation, suspension of organization membership, travel and asset restrictions on targeted persons, "naming and shaming," and other such actions.

3.27 *Economic* direct prevention measures may again include positive as well as negative inducements. Positive inducements might include promises of new funding or investment, or the promise of more favourable trade terms. A distinction must be drawn between regular developmental and humanitarian assistance programmes, on the one hand, and those implemented as a preventive or peace building response to problems that could lead to the outbreak or recurrence of violent conflict, on the other: special care is required to ensure that such assistance helps to prevent or alleviate conflict issues, and does not exacerbate them. Economic direct prevention efforts may also be of a more coercive nature, including threats of trade and financial sanctions; withdrawal of investment; threats to withdraw IMF or World Bank support; and the curtailment of aid and other assistance.

3.28 A spectrum of direct prevention measures of a more *legal* nature can also be employed. On the one hand, these measures might include offers of mediation, or arbitration, or perhaps adjudication – though in cases of domestic dispute these options may not be readily available or acceptable to all parties. The deployment of monitors to observe compliance with human rights standards, and help reassure communities or groups feeling themselves at risk, is another measure that might usefully be considered.

3.29 The threat to seek or apply international legal sanctions has in recent years become a major new weapon in the international preventive armoury. In the first place, the establishment of specialist tribunals to deal with war crimes committed in specific conflicts – for the former Yugoslavia, Rwanda and most recently Sierra Leone – will concentrate the minds of potential perpetrators of crimes against humanity on the risks they run of international retribution.

3.30 Secondly, the establishment of the International Criminal Court – when 60 states have ratified the 1998 Statute – will mean there is new jurisdiction over a wide range of established crimes against humanity and war crimes, some of which are described in greater detail in the Statute than in existing instruments, such as the categories of sexual violence constituting crimes against humanity, and some of which are new, such as the prohibition on the enlistment of child soldiers. The establishment of the International Criminal Court is also to be welcomed as a measure to avoid the accusations of double standards, or "victor's justice," which are periodically aimed at the specialist tribunals just referred to.

3.31 Apart from these international courts, present or planned, the Geneva Conventions and Additional Protocols (as well as the Convention Against Torture) establish universal jurisdiction over crimes listed in them. This means that any state party can bring to trial any person accused of such crimes. Universal jurisdiction is in any case held to exist under customary international law for genocide and crimes against humanity, and a number of countries have enacted legislation to give their courts jurisdiction in such cases. While these provisions have in the past usually been more honoured in the breach than in the observance, the prosecution and conviction in 2001 in a Belgian court of Rwandan nuns charged with complicity in the Rwandan genocide are an indication that the universal jurisdiction of these instruments is starting to be taken very seriously. Another important legal development occurred with the British House of Lords decision in 1998–99 in the General Pinochet extradition case, which went a long way to void the sovereign immunity of government leaders for crimes against humanity committed while they were in office.

3.32   The scope for direct prevention measures of a *military* nature are more limited, but nonetheless important to mention. This might include stand-off reconnaissance, or in particular a consensual preventive deployment of which the UN Preventive Deployment Force (UNPREDEP) in Macedonia is the clearest example to date, and a successful one. In extreme cases, direct prevention might involve the threat to use force.

3.33   The move in each case from incentives for prevention to more intrusive and coercive preventive measures, such as threats of economic sanctions or military measures, is a significant one and should never be undertaken lightly. Such actions may result in the application of very high levels of political and economic – and in extreme cases military – pressure, and to that extent will require a relatively high level of political commitment on the part of the external actors. The use of threats and other coercive measures is also much more likely to engender greater political resistance from the targeted state than would prevention based on positive inducements. Nonetheless, tough threatened direct prevention efforts can be important in eliminating the need to actually resort to coercive measures, including the use of force.

3.34   One of the increasingly evident problems with the whole strategy of prevention is that some states are becoming reluctant to accept any internationally endorsed preventive measures at all – even of the softest and most supportive kind. Their fear is that any "internationalization" of the problem will result in further external "interference" and start down a slippery slope to intervention. There are two answers to this fear. The first is for international policy makers to be sensitive to it: to recognize that many preventive measures are inherently coercive and intrusive in character, to acknowledge that frankly, and to make a very clear distinction between carrots and sticks, taking care always in the first instance to fashion measures that will be non-intrusive and sensitive to national prerogatives. But the second answer is one for the states themselves: those who wish to resist external efforts to help may well, in so doing, increase the risk of inducing increased external involvement, the application of more coercive measures, and in extreme cases, external military intervention. Intervention should only be considered when prevention fails – and the best way of avoiding intervention is to ensure that it doesn't fail.

3.35   Another difficulty that can arise with internationally endorsed and externally applied preventive measures is that political leaders facing internal rebellion or secessionist violence will often be concerned about giving additional momentum or "legitimacy" to those causing their problems. Those concerns should be understood and appreciated, and a careful evaluation always made of the risks of well-intentioned efforts in fact making the situation worse. It is also critical in this regard that those wanting to help from outside completely recognize and respect the sovereignty and territorial integrity of the countries concerned, and confine their efforts to finding solutions within those parameters. We make this point again in Chapter 5, in discussing the follow-up to military intervention, that the objective overall is not to change constitutional arrangements or undermine sovereignty, but to protect them.

3.36   Effective conflict prevention depends on disparate actors working together strategically. States, the UN and its specialized agencies, the international financial institutions, regional organizations, NGOs, religious groups, the business community, the media, and scientific, professional and educational communities all have a role to play. The capacity to conduct preventive diplomacy ultimately relies on the international ability to coordinate multilateral initiatives, and identify logical divisions of labour. The mention of "coordination" normally makes eyes glaze, but the issue is one of perennial concern. The number of coordinating committees and meetings is large, but they do not necessarily improve coordination. It is obvious that states and non-state organizations often have varying interests and agendas; and in zones of potentially catastrophic conflict where external actors have significant interests (and usually more than a few rivalries), coordination of preventive actions can be especially difficult. This provides easy ammunition for indigenous actors to exploit divisions among external players. When this reality is combined with the need to coordinate and create divisions of labour across agencies and to be flexible in sequencing preventive measures over time, the prospects for strategic coherence are formidable.

3.37   It is important to have an operational strategy, of the kind that has been proposed by the Carnegie Commission among others, for direct prevention efforts. It is desirable to have a lead player to manage multi-actor prevention, and to avoid the prospect of prevention by committee and all the strategic incoherence that implies. It is important to be able to integrate quick-impact development projects into diplomatic initiatives. It would be highly desirable to have available a pool of unrestricted development funds for use by a third party at very short notice – a capacity that does not presently exist within the UN, and has long been a major constraint on the ability of mediators to "sweeten the pot" for parties to a dispute and to engage in even rudimentary confidence building measures.

3.38   The media have a particularly important role in conflict prevention, in particular in alerting policy makers – and the public opinion that influences them – to the catastrophic consequences that so often flow from no action being taken. More immediate and more graphic stories will always tend to take precedence, but there is much more that can and should be done to identify emerging issues, explain the human risks associated with them, and prod decision makers into appropriate action.

3.39   Conflict prevention must be integrated into policies, planning and programmes at the national, regional and international levels. Member states should be asked to give the Secretary-General regular reports and updates on capacities, capabilities and current practices designed to prevent conflict – at the national level and as part of a contribution to global conflict prevention efforts. Regional and sub-regional organizations should also contribute their experiences and plans to this global effort – making the UN the repository of best practice tools and strategies. The effective prevention of conflict requires, in particular, that development, foreign policy, finance and defence ministry dimensions of conflict prevention efforts be drawn together. Both donors and recipients should begin to structure their approach to conflict prevention in a way that ensures coherence, continuity of effort and real impact.

3.40   The Commission strongly believes that it is critical that more resources, more energy, more competence and more commitment be put into prevention. Time and time again attention has been drawn to the need for stronger and more effective prevention efforts – most recently by the Secretary-General in his well received and much debated recent report to the General Assembly and Security Council – yet the tangible commitment to prevention remains weak. Moving from talk to action means greater willingness on the part of local and national communities to take the kinds of steps that are required if conflict is to be avoided, together with a greater willingness by external actors to ensure that their actions do not serve to make a particular situation worse. It means more active efforts at the sub-regional and regional levels for conflict prevention, and much greater support for these efforts at all levels. It means a serious focus within the UN system on ensuring that information is transformed into concrete and practical analysis. It means a broader determination overall to ensure that early warning translates into early action.

3.41   Good conflict prevention behaviour by states that are still fragile and emerging from conflict, or in conflict-prone areas, must be encouraged, supported and rewarded by the international community in practical ways. The World Bank and IMF should work together with the UN and regional or sub-regional organizations to ensure that full support is given to these states that have made concerted efforts to deal with governance, reconciliation and long-term rehabilitation and reconstruction issues. Specific, tailored support should be offered, on an urgent basis, by the international community to consolidate these efforts. Using the UN as a focal point, an integrated Task Force could be established which would draw together UN, Bretton Woods and appropriate regional, sub-regional and national institutions to develop specific strategies to provide for the rapid recognition of such efforts, and to design tailored assistance packages which go well beyond traditional aid to deal with longer term sustainability issues such as trade and investment and institution building.

3.42   Underlying all the specifics, what is necessary is for the international community to change its basic mindset from a "culture of reaction" to that of a "culture of prevention." To create such a culture will mean, as the Secretary-General reminds us, "setting standards for accountability of member states and contributing to the establishing of prevention practices at the local, national, regional and global levels." It is a task long overdue.

3.43   Without a genuine commitment to conflict prevention at all levels – without new energy and momentum being devoted to the task – the world will continue to witness the needless slaughter of our fellow human beings, and the reckless waste of precious resources on conflict rather than social and economic development. The time has come for all of us to take practical responsibility to prevent the needless loss of human life, and to be ready to act in the cause of prevention and not just in the aftermath of disaster.

4. THE RESPONSIBILITY TO REACT

4.1   The "responsibility to protect" implies above all else a responsibility to react to situations of compelling need for human protection. When preventive measures fail to resolve or contain the situation and when a state is unable or unwilling to redress the situation, then interventionary measures by other members of the broader community of states may be required. These coercive measures may include political, economic or judicial measures, and in extreme cases – but only extreme cases – they may also include military action. As a matter of first principles, in the case of reaction just as with prevention, less intrusive and coercive measures should always be considered before more coercive and intrusive ones are applied.

4.2   Tough threshold conditions should be satisfied before military intervention is contemplated. For political, economic and judicial measures the barrier can be set lower, but for military intervention it must be high: for military action ever to be defensible the circumstances must be grave indeed. But the threshold or "trigger" conditions are not the end of the matter. There are a series of additional precautionary principles which must be satisfied, to ensure that the intervention remains both defensible in principle and workable and acceptable in practice.

MEASURES SHORT OF MILITARY ACTION

4.3   The failure of either root cause or direct prevention measures to stave off or contain a humanitarian crisis or conflict does not mean that military action is necessarily required. Wherever possible, coercive measures short of military intervention ought first to be examined, including in particular various types of political, economic and military sanctions.

4.4   Sanctions inhibit the capacity of states to interact with the outside world, while not physically preventing the state from carrying out actions within its borders. Such measures still aim to persuade the authorities concerned to take or not take particular action or actions. Military intervention, on the other hand, directly interferes with the capacity of a domestic authority to operate on its own territory. It effectively displaces the domestic authority and aims (at least in the short term) to address directly the particular problem or threat that has arisen. For these reasons, and because of the inherent risks that accompany any use of deadly force, the prospect of coercive military action has always raised broader and more intense concerns than has the imposition of political, diplomatic or economic sanctions.

4.5   Although the use of coercive measures short of military force is generally preferable to the use of force, these non-military measures can be blunt and often indiscriminate weapons and must be used with extreme care to avoid doing more harm than good – especially to civilian populations. Blanket economic sanctions in particular have been increasingly discredited in recent years as many have noted that the hardships exacted upon the civilian population by such sanctions tend to be greatly disproportionate to the likely impact of the sanctions on the behaviour of the principal players. Such sanctions also tend quickly to develop holes and deteriorate further over time, not least when they are poorly monitored, as has been almost universally the case. Sanctions that target leadership groups and security organizations responsible for gross human rights violations have emerged as an increasingly important alternative to general sanctions in recent years, and efforts to make such sanctions more effective have drawn increasing attention. A standard exemption for food and medical supplies is now generally recognized by the Security Council and under international law, though the issue of the provision of medical supplies to combatants may sometimes still generate debate.

4.6   Efforts to target sanctions more effectively so as to decrease the impact on innocent civilians and increase the impact on decision makers have been focused in three different areas, military, economic and political/diplomatic. In all three areas, effective monitoring is crucial if the measures are to have any prospect of being effective.

4.7   In the military area:

❑ Arms embargoes are an important tool of the Security Council and the international community when conflict arises or is threatened. Such embargoes generally include the sale of military equipment as well as spare parts.

❑ Ending military cooperation and training programmes is another common, if less strenuous, measure used or threatened by states to bring about compliance with international norms, though results can vary.

4.8   In the economic area:

❑ Financial sanctions may target the foreign assets of a country, or a rebel movement or terrorist organization, or the foreign assets of particular leaders. Where individuals are targeted, these efforts have increasingly been expanded also to include members of that individual's immediate family.

❑ Restrictions on income generating activities such as oil, diamonds and logging and drugs, have more and more come to be regarded as one of the most important types of targeted sanctions, because such activities are generally easier to get at than the funds that they generate, and because the profits from such activities are often not just a means to start or sustain a conflict but in many cases the principal motivation for the conflict.

❑ Restrictions on access to petroleum products can be an important way of restricting military operations, though such restrictions may also have a broad and possibly devastating impact on civilians and the local economy.

❑ Aviation bans have been used in a number of cases and generally prohibit international air traffic to or from a particular destination.

4.9   In the political and diplomatic area:

❑ Restrictions on diplomatic representation, including expulsion of staff, while often viewed in the past as primarily of symbolic significance and largely related to the battle for public opinion, have also increasingly come to be seen as a relevant and useful measure in efforts to limit illicit transactions – whether for the sale of illicit commodities such as illegally mined diamonds or drugs or for the purchase of arms and other military related materiel, or with respect to the movement of funds.

❑ Restrictions on travel, not least to major international shopping destinations, have proved to have some utility when against specific leaders or individuals and their families.

❑ Suspension of membership or expulsion from international or regional bodies, and the loss this may entail not only of national prestige, but also of technical cooperation or financial assistance countries may receive from such bodies, is another increasingly used tool.

❑ Refusal to admit a country to membership of a body is a corollary of the foregoing which has sometimes been employed to good·effect.

THE DECISION TO INTERVENE

Extreme Cases Only

4.10   In extreme and exceptional cases, the responsibility to react may involve the need to resort to military action. But what is an extreme case? Where should we draw the line in determining when military intervention is, prima facie, defensible?

4.11   The starting point, here as elsewhere, should be the principle of non-intervention. This is the norm from which any departure has to be justified. All members of the United Nations have an interest in maintaining an order of sovereign, self-reliant, responsible, yet interdependent states. In most situations, this interest is best served if all states, large and small, abstain from intervening or interfering in the domestic affairs of other states. Most internal political or civil disagreements, even conflicts, within states do not require coercive intervention by external powers. The non-interference rule not only protects states and governments: it also protects peoples and cultures, enabling societies to maintain the religious, ethnic, and civilizational differences that they cherish.

4.12   The norm of non-intervention is the equivalent in international affairs of the Hippocratic principle – first do no harm. Intervention in the domestic affairs of states is often harmful. It can destabilize the order of states, while fanning ethnic or civil strife. When internal forces seeking to oppose a state believe that they can generate outside support by mounting campaigns of violence, the internal order of all states is potentially compromised. The rule against intervention in internal affairs encourages states to solve their own internal problems and prevent these from spilling over into a threat to international peace and security.

4.13   Yet there are exceptional circumstances in which the very interest that all states have in maintaining a stable international order requires them to react when all order within a state has broken down or when civil conflict and repression are so violent that civilians are threatened with massacre, genocide or ethnic cleansing on a large scale. The Commission found in its consultations that even in states where there was the strongest opposition to infringements on sovereignty, there was general acceptance that there must be limited exceptions to the non-intervention rule for certain kinds of emergencies. Generally expressed, the view was that these exceptional circumstances must be cases of violence which so genuinely "shock the conscience of mankind," or which present such a clear and present danger to international security, that they require coercive military intervention.

4.14   Given this broad international agreement on the need, in exceptional cases of human risk, for coercive military action across borders, the task is to define, with as much precision as possible, what these exceptional circumstances are, so as to maximize the chances of consensus being reached in any given case. What is the precise threshold of violence and abuse or other violation that must be crossed before coercive military force across a national border can begin to be justified? Are there any other criteria which should or must be satisfied before the decision to intervene is made?

Six Criteria for Military Intervention

4.15   It is perhaps not as difficult as it appears at first sight to identify criteria for military intervention for human protection purposes about which people should be able to agree. It is true that there are presently almost as many different lists of such criteria as there are contributions to the literature and political debate on this subject. But the differing length of these lists, and the different terminology involved, should not obscure the reality that there is an enormous amount of common ground to be found when one focuses on the core issues.

4.16   While there is no universally accepted single list, in the Commission's judgement all the relevant decision making criteria can be succinctly summarized under the following six headings: *right authority, just cause, right intention, last resort, proportional means* and *reasonable prospects.*

4.17   The element of *right authority* – who can authorize a military intervention – is a critical one, and deserves a full discussion to itself: it gets this in Chapter 6. The content of the *just cause* principle – what kind of harm is sufficient to trigger a military intervention overriding the non-intervention principle – is the other question requiring most discussion, and is the subject of the next section of this chapter. The remaining four criteria, each adding a different element of prudence or precaution to the decision making equation, are discussed together in the last section of this chapter.

THRESHOLD CRITERIA: JUST CAUSE

4.18   Calls for intervention for human protection purposes have in the past been made on a wide range and variety of grounds, involving and in response to a wide range of circumstances and conditions, and many different criteria for intervention were suggested during the course of our consultations. The Commission's view is that exceptions to the principle of non-intervention should be limited. Military intervention for human protection purposes must be regarded as an exceptional and extraordinary measure, and for it to be warranted, there must be serious and irreparable harm occurring to human beings, or imminently likely to occur.

4.19   In the Commission's view, military intervention for human protection purposes is justified in two broad sets of circumstances, namely in order to halt or avert:

- ❑ *large scale loss of life, actual or apprehended, with genocidal intent or not, which is the product either of deliberate state action, or state neglect or inability to act, or a failed state situation; or*

- ❑ *large scale "ethnic cleansing," actual or apprehended, whether carried out by killing, forced expulsion, acts of terror or rape.*

If either or both of these conditions are satisfied, it is our view that the "just cause" component of the decision to intervene is amply satisfied.

4.20   It is important to make clear both what these two conditions include and what they exclude. In the Commission's view, these conditions would typically *include* the following types of conscience-shocking situation:

- ❑ those actions defined by the framework of the 1948 Genocide Convention that involve large scale threatened or actual loss of life;

- ❑ the threat or occurrence of large scale loss of life, whether the product of genocidal intent or not, and whether or not involving state action;

- ❑ different manifestations of "ethnic cleansing," including the systematic killing of members of a particular group in order to diminish or eliminate their presence in a particular area; the systematic physical removal of members of a particular group from a particular geographical area; acts of terror designed to force people to flee; and the systematic rape for political purposes of women of a particular group (either as another form of terrorism, or as a means of changing the ethnic composition of that group);

- ❑ those crimes against humanity and violations of the laws of war, as defined in the Geneva Conventions and Additional Protocols and elsewhere, which involve large scale killing or ethnic cleansing;

- ❑ situations of state collapse and the resultant exposure of the population to mass starvation and/or civil war; and

- ❑ overwhelming natural or environmental catastrophes, where the state concerned is either unwilling or unable to cope, or call for assistance, and significant loss of life is occurring or threatened.

4.21   In both the broad conditions we identified – loss of life and ethnic cleansing – we have described the action in question as needing to be "large scale" in order to justify military intervention. We make no attempt to quantify "large scale": opinions may differ in some marginal cases (for example, where a number of small scale incidents may build cumulatively into large scale atrocity), but most will not in practice generate major disagreement. What we do make clear, however, is that military action can be legitimate as an anticipatory measure in response to clear evidence of likely large scale killing. Without this possibility of anticipatory action, the international community would be placed in the morally untenable position of being required to wait until genocide begins, before being able to take action to stop it.

4.22   The principles we have specified do not attempt to draw a distinction between situations where the killing or ethnic cleansing is caused by the action – or deliberate inaction – of a state, and those where the state in question has failed or collapsed. In a failed or collapsed state situation, with no government effectively able to exercise the sovereign responsibility of protecting its people, the principle of non-intervention might seem to have less force. But when it comes to the threshold "just cause" issue of determining whether the circumstances are grave enough to justify intervention, it makes no basic moral difference whether it is state or non-state actors who are putting people at risk.

4.23   Again, the principles as we have defined them make no distinction between those abuses occurring wholly within state borders, with no immediate cross-border consequences, and those with wider repercussions. This reflects our confidence that, in extreme conscience-shocking cases of the kind with which we are concerned, the element of threat to international peace and security, required under Chapter VII of the Charter as a precondition for Security Council authorization of military intervention, will be usually found to exist. Security Council practice in the 1990s indicates that the Council is already prepared to authorize coercive deployments in cases where the crisis in question is, for all practical purposes, confined within the borders of a particular state.

4.24 While our "just cause" conditions are broadly framed, the Commission also makes clear that they exclude some situations which have been claimed from time to time to justify the coercive use of military force for human protection purposes.

4.25 First, the Commission has resisted any temptation to identify as a ground for military intervention human rights violations falling short of outright killing or ethnic cleansing, for example systematic racial discrimination, or the systematic imprisonment or other repression of political opponents. These may be eminently appropriate cases for considering the application of political, economic or military sanctions, but they do not in the Commission's view justify military action for human protection purposes.

4.26 Secondly, the Commission has taken a similar view in relation to cases where a population, having clearly expressed its desire for a democratic regime, is denied its democratic rights by a military take-over. The overthrow of a democratic government is a grave matter, requiring concerted international action such as sanctions and suspension or withdrawal of credits, international membership and recognition – and there might well be wider regional security implications such that the Security Council is prepared to authorize military intervention (including by a regional organization) on traditional "international peace and security" grounds. There may also be situations where the overthrown government expressly requests military support, and that could clearly be given within the scope of the self-defence provisions in Article 51 of the UN Charter. But the Commission's view is that military intervention for human protection purposes should be restricted exclusively, here as elsewhere, to those situations where large scale loss of civilian life or ethnic cleansing is threatened or taking place.

4.27 Thirdly, as to the use of military force by a state to rescue its own nationals on foreign territory, sometimes claimed as another justification for "humanitarian intervention," we regard that as being again a matter appropriately covered under existing international law, and in particular Article 51 of the UN Charter. The same goes for the use of force in response to a terrorist attack on a state's territory and citizens: to the extent that military action is justified, it would be supported by a combination of Article 51 and the general provisions of Chapter VII, as the Security Council has now made clear with its resolutions in the aftermath of 11 September 2001.

The Question of Evidence

4.28 Even where consensus has been reached on the types of situations which might warrant a military intervention, it will still be necessary in each case to determine whether events on the ground do in fact meet the criteria presented – actual or threatened large scale loss of human life or ethnic cleansing. In many cases, competing "facts" and versions of events will be produced – often for the specific purpose of leading or misleading external opinion. Obtaining fair and accurate information is difficult but essential.

4.29 Ideally there would be a report as to the gravity of the situation, and the inability or unwillingness of the state in question to manage it satisfactorily, from a universally respected and impartial non-government source. The International Committee for the Red

Cross (ICRC) is an obvious candidate for this role, often mentioned to us, but for understandable reasons – based on the necessity for it to remain, and be seen to remain, absolutely removed from political decision making, and able to operate anywhere on the ground – it is absolutely unwilling to take on any such role.

4.30   It is difficult to conceive of any institutional solution to the problem of evidence, of a kind that would put the satisfaction of the "just cause" criterion absolutely beyond doubt or argument in every case. But there are other ways in which credible information and assessments can be obtained, and the evidence allowed to speak for itself. Reports prepared in the normal course of their operations by or for UN organs and agencies – such as the High Commissioners for Human Rights and for Refugees – are important, as can be assessments made for their own purposes by other credible international organizations and non-governmental organizations, and on occasion the media.

4.31   Moreover, where existence of the conditions that might warrant an intervention for human protection purposes is in question, and time allows, an independent special fact-finding mission could be sent by the Security Council or the Secretary-General for the purpose of obtaining accurate information and a fair assessment of a particular situation. The Commission believes there is particular utility in the Secretary-General seeking the advice of well-placed objective witnesses and others highly knowledgeable about the situation in question. The Secretary-General of the UN has formidable, but hitherto much underutilized, authority under Article 99 of the Charter to "bring to the attention of the Security Council any matter which in his opinion may threaten the maintenance of inter-national peace and security": it is a power that could be utilized to extremely influential effect in the present context.

OTHER PRECAUTIONARY CRITERIA

4.32   For a military intervention decision to be, and be seen to be, justified, there are four other substantial conditions that have to be met at the outset: right intention, last resort, proportional means and reasonable prospects. When both these and the threshold "just cause" principle are taken together, to jointly shape the policy decisions of both the Security Council and member states, the Commission believes that they will strictly limit the use of coercive military force for human protection purposes. Our purpose is not to license aggression with fine words, or to provide strong states with new rationales for doubtful strategic designs, but to strengthen the order of states by providing for clear guidelines to guide concerted international action in those exceptional circumstances when violence within a state menaces all peoples.

Right Intention

4.33   The primary purpose of the intervention must be to halt or avert human suffering. Any use of military force that aims from the outset, for example, for the alteration of borders or the advancement of a particular combatant group's claim to self-determination, cannot be justified. Overthrow of regimes is not, as such, a legitimate objective, although disabling that regime's capacity to harm its own people may be essential to discharging the mandate of protection – and what is necessary to achieve that disabling will vary from case to case. Occupation of territory may not be able to be avoided, but it should not be an objective as such, and there should be a clear commitment from the outset to returning the territory to its sovereign owner at the conclusion of hostilities or, if that is not possible, administering it on an interim basis under UN auspices.

4.34   One way of helping ensure that the "right intention" criterion is satisfied is to have military intervention always take place on a collective or multilateral rather than single-country basis. Another is to look to whether, and to what extent, the intervention is actually supported by the people for whose benefit the intervention is intended. Another is to look to whether, and to what extent, the opinion of other countries in the region has been taken into account and is supportive. In some discussions these considerations are identified as separate criteria in their own right, but the Commission's view is that they should be regarded as sub-components of the larger element of right intention.

4.35   It may not always be the case that the humanitarian motive is the *only* one moving the intervening state or states, even within the framework of Security Council-authorized intervention. Complete disinterestedness – the absence of any narrow self-interest at all – may be an ideal, but it is not likely always to be a reality: mixed motives, in international relations as everywhere else, are a fact of life. Moreover, the budgetary cost and risk to personnel involved in any military action may in fact make it politically imperative for the intervening state to be able to claim some degree of self-interest in the intervention, however altruistic its primary motive might actually be. Apart from economic or strategic interests, that self-interest could, for example, take the understandable form of a concern to avoid refugee outflows, or a haven for drug producers or terrorists, developing in one's neighbourhood.

4.36   To those domestic constituencies who may actually demand of their governments, when it comes to intervention for human protection purposes, that they *not* be altruistic, or moved by what we have called "right intention," and that they should have regard only to their own country's national interests, the best short answer may be that, these days, good international citizenship is a matter of national self-interest. With the world as close and interdependent as it now is, and with crises in "faraway countries of which we know little" as capable as they now are of generating major problems elsewhere (with refugee outflows, health pandemics, terrorism, narcotics trafficking, organized crime and the like), it is strongly arguable that it is in every country's interest to contribute cooperatively to the resolution of such problems, quite apart from the humanitarian imperative to do so. This is a theme to which we will return in our concluding chapter.

Last Resort

4.37   Every diplomatic and non-military avenue for the prevention or peaceful resolution of the humanitarian crisis must have been explored. The responsibility to react – with military coercion – can only be justified when the responsibility to prevent has been fully discharged. This does not necessarily mean that every such option must literally have been tried and failed: often there will simply not be the time for that process to work itself out. But it does mean that there must be reasonable grounds for believing that, in all the circumstances, if the measure had been attempted it would not have succeeded.

4.38   If the crisis in question involves a conflict between a state party and an insurgent minority, the parties must be induced to negotiate. Ceasefires, followed, if necessary, by the deployment of international peacekeepers and observers are always a better option, if possible, than coercive military responses. The long-term solution for ethnic minority conflict or secessionist pressures within a state will often be some kind of devolutionist compromise that guarantees the minority its linguistic, political and cultural autonomy, while preserving the integrity of the state in question. Only when good faith attempts to find such compromises, monitored or brokered by the international community, founder on the intransigence of one or both parties, and full-scale violence is in prospect or in occurrence, can a military option by outside powers be considered.

Proportional Means

4.39 The scale, duration and intensity of the planned military intervention should be the minimum necessary to secure the humanitarian objective in question. The means have to be commensurate with the ends, and in line with the magnitude of the original provocation. The effect on the political system of the country targeted should be limited, again, to what is strictly necessary to accomplish the purpose of the intervention. While it may be a matter for argument in each case what are the precise practical implications of these strictures, the principles involved are clear enough.

4.40 It should go without saying that all the rules of international humanitarian law should be strictly observed in these situations. Indeed, since military intervention involves a form of military action significantly more narrowly focused and targeted than all out warfighting, an argument can be made that even higher standards should apply in these cases.

Reasonable Prospects

4.41 Military action can only be justified if it stands a reasonable chance of success, that is, halting or averting the atrocities or suffering that triggered the intervention in the first place. Military intervention is not justified if actual protection cannot be achieved, or if the consequences of embarking upon the intervention are likely to be worse than if there is no action at all. In particular, a military action for limited human protection purposes cannot be justified if in the process it triggers a larger conflict. It will be the case that some human beings simply cannot be rescued except at unacceptable cost – perhaps of a larger regional conflagration, involving major military powers. In such cases, however painful the reality, coercive military action is no longer justified.

4.42 Application of this precautionary principle would on purely utilitarian grounds be likely to preclude military action against any one of the five permanent members of the Security Council even if all the other conditions for intervention described here were met. It is difficult to imagine a major conflict being avoided, or success in the original objective being achieved, if such action were mounted against any of them. The same is true of other major powers who are not permanent members of Security Council. This raises again the question of double standards – but the Commission's position here, as elsewhere, is simply this: the reality that interventions may not be able to be mounted in every case where there is justification for doing so, is no reason for them not to be mounted in any case.

4.43 In relation to the major powers, there are still other types of pressure that can be applied, as happened, for example, in the case of Indonesia and East Timor. And other types of collective action – including sanctions – could and should still be considered in such cases as part of the responsibility to protect.

5. THE RESPONSIBILITY TO REBUILD

POST-INTERVENTION OBLIGATIONS

Peace Building

5.1   The responsibility to protect implies the responsibility not just to prevent and react, but to follow through and rebuild. This means that if military intervention action is taken – because of a breakdown or abdication of a state's own capacity and authority in discharging its "responsibility to protect" – there should be a genuine commitment to helping to build a durable peace, and promoting good governance and sustainable development. Conditions of public safety and order have to be reconstituted by international agents acting in partnership with local authorities, with the goal of progressively transferring to them authority and responsibility to rebuild.

5.2   Ensuring sustainable reconstruction and rehabilitation will involve the commitment of sufficient funds and resources and close cooperation with local people, and may mean staying in the country for some period of time after the initial purposes of the intervention have been accomplished. Too often in the past the responsibility to rebuild has been insufficiently recognized, the exit of the interveners has been poorly managed, the commitment to help with reconstruction has been inadequate, and countries have found themselves at the end of the day still wrestling with the underlying problems that produced the original intervention action.

5.3   If military intervention is to be contemplated, the need for a post-intervention strategy is also of paramount importance. Military intervention is one instrument in a broader spectrum of tools designed to prevent conflicts and humanitarian emergencies from arising, intensifying, spreading, persisting or recurring. The objective of such a strategy must be to help ensure that the conditions that prompted the military intervention do not repeat themselves or simply resurface.

5.4   The most successful reconciliation processes do not necessarily occur at high level political dialogue tables, or in judicial-style processes (though we well understand the positive role that truth and reconciliation commissions can play in certain post-conflict environments). True reconciliation is best generated by ground level reconstruction efforts, when former armed adversaries join hands in rebuilding their community or creating reasonable living and job conditions at new settlements. True and lasting reconciliation occurs with sustained daily efforts at repairing infrastructure, at rebuilding housing, at planting and harvesting, and cooperating in other productive activities. External support for reconciliation efforts must be conscious of the need to encourage this cooperation, and dynamically linked to joint development efforts between former adversaries.

5.5   The Secretary-General described very clearly the nature of and rationale for post-conflict peace building in his 1998 report on *The Causes of Conflict and the Promotion of Durable Peace and Sustainable Development in Africa:*

> By post-conflict peace-building, I mean actions undertaken at the end of a conflict to consolidate peace and prevent a recurrence of armed confrontation. Experience has shown that the consolidation of peace in the aftermath of conflict requires more than purely diplomatic and military action, and that an integrated peace-building effort is needed to address the various factors which have caused or are threatening a conflict. Peace-building may involve the creation or strengthening of national institutions, monitoring elections, promoting human rights, providing for reintegration and rehabilitation programmes, as well as creating conditions for resumed development. Peace-building does not replace ongoing humanitarian and development activities in countries emerging from crises. Rather it aims to build on, add to, or reorient such activities in ways that are designed to reduce the risk of a resumption of conflict and contribute to creating conditions most conducive to reconciliation, reconstruction and recovery.

5.6   The Secretary-General's report goes on to describe in more detail what is needed in the aftermath of conflict, or in this case intervention:

> Societies which have emerged from conflict have special needs. To avoid a return to conflict while laying a solid foundation for development, emphasis must be placed on critical priorities such as encouraging reconciliation and demonstrating respect for human rights; fostering political inclusiveness and promoting national unity; ensuring the safe, smooth and early repatriation and resettlement of refugees and displaced persons; reintegrating ex-combatants and others into productive society; curtailing the availability of small arms; and mobilizing the domestic and international resources for reconstruction and economic recovery. Each priority is linked to every other, and success will require a concerted and coordinated effort on all fronts.

The message is clear. There is no substitute for a clear and effective post-intervention strategy.

5.7   In what follows, we briefly review some of the main issues that confront policy makers in exercising the responsibility to rebuild in the three most immediately crucial areas of security, justice and economic development. In Chapter 7, dealing with operational issues, we revisit a number of these matters from the perspective of the military forces on the ground in post-intervention environments.

Security

5.8   One of the essential functions of an intervention force is to provide basic security and protection for all members of a population, regardless of ethnic origin or relation to the previous source of power in the territory. In post-conflict situations, revenge killings and even "reverse ethnic cleansing" frequently occur as groups who were victimized attack groups associated with their former oppressors. It is essential that post-intervention operations plan for this contingency before entry and provide effective security for all populations, regardless of origin, once entry occurs. There can be no such thing as "guilty minorities" in the post-intervention phase. Everyone is entitled to basic protection for their lives and property.

5.9   One of the most difficult and important issues to be regularly confronted in the post-intervention phase relates to the *disarmament, demobilization and reintegration* of local security forces. Reintegration will usually take the longest time to achieve, but the whole process cannot be judged to have been successful until it is complete. It is also a necessary element of returning a country to law and order since a demobilized soldier, unless properly reintegrated into society, with sustainable income, will probably turn to armed crime or armed political opposition. Successful disarmament of personnel from military and security forces, and other efforts to collect small arms and curb the entry of new ones, will be an important element of this effort.

5.10   Another element of the same problem is the rebuilding of new national armed forces and police, integrating as far as possible elements of the formerly competing armed factions or military forces. This process will be vital to national reconciliation and protection of the re-established state once the intervening forces leave. However, all too often in the past, in Cambodia and elsewhere, it has proved to be too long-term for the intervening authorities, and too expensive and sensitive for international donors who wish to avoid later accusations of re-arming former enemies.

5.11   Complaints are regularly heard from military officers around the world that in interventions and their aftermath they are all too often given functions for which they are not trained and which are more appropriate to police. The simple answer is that civilian police are really only able to operate in countries where functioning systems of law and courts exist. Although the presence of some police in any military operation may be necessary from the start, including for the purpose of training local police, there is probably little alternative to the current practice of deploying largely military forces at the start, but as conditions improve and governmental institutions are rebuilt, phasing in a civilian police presence.

5.12   An essential part of pre-intervention planning has been identified by both political and military personnel as being an *exit strategy* (not the same thing as an exit timetable) for intervening troops. There is force in the argument that without such a strategy there are serious risks in mounting any military intervention at all, as an unplanned, let alone precipitate, exit could have disastrous, or at best unsettling, implications for the country, and could also serve to discredit even the positive aspects of the intervention itself.

Justice and Reconciliation

5.13   In many cases the country in which a military intervention takes place may never have enjoyed a non-corrupt or properly functioning *judicial system*, including both the courts and police, or this may have deteriorated or disappeared as the state itself began to fail. Increasingly, and particularly from the time of the UN Transitional Authority in Cambodia (UNTAC) in the early 1990s, there has been a realization in UN circles and elsewhere about the importance of making transitional arrangements for justice during an operation, and restoring judicial systems as soon as possible thereafter. The point is simply that if an intervening force has a mandate to guard against further human rights violations, but there is no functioning system to bring violators to justice, then not only is the force's mandate to that extent unachievable, but its whole operation is likely to have diminished credibility both locally and internationally.

5.14 A number of non-governmental bodies have developed "justice packages," which can be adapted to the specific conditions of a wide variety of operations, and these should be considered an integral part of any post-intervention peace building strategy, pending the re-establishment of local institutions. Such measures should include a standard model penal code, able to be used in any situation where there is no appropriate existing body of law to apply, and applied immediately the intervention begins to ensure protection of minorities and allow intervening forces to detain persons committing crimes.

5.15 A related issue is that of the return of refugees and the *legal rights of returnees* from ethnic or other minorities. Unequal treatment in the provision of basic services, repatriation assistance and employment, and property laws, are often designed to send a powerful signal that returnees are not welcome. Discrimination in the provision of reconstruction assistance has been a major problem in Croatia, for instance, where it was enshrined in law. In many cases around the world, attempts by returnees to use the courts to evict temporary occupants (often themselves refugees) from their homes and regain rightful property have ended in frustration rather than re-possession. Laws either provide inadequate protection of property rights or were framed to deter potential returnees and disadvantage those who do return.

5.16 Barriers include difficulties in establishing tenancy rights over formerly socially-owned property, the main form of property holding in former Yugoslavia, for example; the absence of legal documentation; and continued obstructionism by local authorities. The problem of refugees and internally displaced persons (IDPs) seeking to reclaim their property has been particularly acute in urban areas. Political pressure to relocate other families in vacated premises has often obstructed returns and little progress has been made in revising the legal rights of urban tenants.

5.17 Facilitating returns requires the removal of the administrative and bureaucratic obstacles to return, ending the culture of impunity vis-à-vis known or suspected war criminals and the adoption of non-discriminatory property laws. However, evictions alone will not solve all the returns issues. A sizeable amount of new housing stock will usually need to be built throughout the country and donor funded projects are critical in meeting these needs.

5.18 Additionally, the question of return sustainability – pivotal to ensuring the long-term success of repatriation – will need to be properly treated. Return sustainability is about creating the right social and economic conditions for returnees. It also includes access to health, education and basic services, and is linked to reform in other areas – eradicating corruption, promoting good governance, and long-term economic regeneration of the country.

Development

5.19 A final peace building responsibility of any military intervention should be as far as possible to encourage economic growth, the recreation of markets and sustainable development. The issues are extremely important, as economic growth not only has law and order implications but is vital to the overall recovery of the country concerned. A consistent corollary of this objective must be for the intervening authorities to find a basis as soon as possible to end any coercive economic measures they may have applied to the country before or during the intervention, and not prolong comprehensive or punitive sanctions.

5.20 Intervening authorities have a particular responsibility to manage as swiftly and smoothly as possible the transfer of development responsibility and project implementation to local leadership, and local actors working with the assistance of national and international development agencies.

5.21 This is not only of importance for long-term development purposes, but also represents a positive reinforcement for short run security measures of the kind discussed above: a positive contribution is provided by a simultaneous effort at training the demobilized for new income generating activities as well as the implementation of social and economic reintegration projects. The sooner the demobilized combatants are aware of their future options and opportunities, and the sooner the community has concrete and tangible demonstrations that civilian life can in fact return to normality under secure conditions, the more positive will be their response in relation to disarmament and related issues.

ADMINISTRATION UNDER UN AUTHORITY

5.22 Useful guidelines for the behaviour of intervening authorities during a military intervention in failed states, and in the follow-up period, might be found in a constructive adaptation of Chapter XII of the UN Charter. This would enable reconstruction and rehabilitation to take place in an orderly way across the full spectrum, with the support and assistance of the international community. The most relevant provision in this regard is Article 76 which notes that the aim of the system is to promote the political, economic, social and educational advancement of the people of the territory in question; to encourage respect for human rights; to ensure the equal treatment of all peoples in the UN in social, economic and commercial matters; and also to ensure equal treatment in the administration of justice.

5.23 A further element of Chapter XII which would often be of relevance to the populations of countries in which an intervention takes place relates to self-determination (Article 76.b). Protective enforcement usually indicates sustaining or restoring forms of territorial self-government and autonomy, and this in turn will usually mean elections being facilitated and possibly supervised, or at least monitored, by the intervening authorities. That said, the responsibility to protect is fundamentally a principle designed to respond to threats to human life, and not a tool for achieving political goals such as greater political autonomy, self-determination, or independence for particular groups within the country (though these underlying issues may well be related to the humanitarian concerns that prompted the military intervention). The intervention itself should not become the basis for further separatist claims.

5.24 There is always likely in the UN to be a generalized resistance to any resurrection of the "trusteeship" concept, on the ground that it represents just another kind of intrusion into internal affairs. But "failed states" are quite likely to generate situations which the international community simply cannot ignore, as happened – although there the intervention was less than successful – in Somalia. The strongest argument against the proposal is probably practical: the cost of such an operation for the necessarily long time it would take to recreate civil society and rehabilitate the infrastructure in such a state. There must be real doubts about the willingness of governments to provide those kinds of resources, other than on a very infrequent and ad hoc basis.

LOCAL OWNERSHIP AND THE LIMITS TO OCCUPATION

5.25   The requirement to stay on in the country in which intervention takes place long enough to ensure sustainable reconstruction and rehabilitation has both positive and negative implications. Apart from, hopefully, removing or at least greatly ameliorating, the root causes of the original conflict and restoring a measure of good governance and economic stability, such a period may also better accustom the population to democratic institutions and processes if these had been previously missing from their country. However, staying on could obviously have some negative aspects, and they are worth spelling out.

Sovereignty

5.26   Sovereignty issues necessarily arise with any continued presence by the intervener in the target country in the follow-up period. Intervention suspends sovereignty claims to the extent that good governance – as well as peace and stability – cannot be promoted or restored unless the intervener has authority over a territory. But the suspension of the exercise of sovereignty is only *de facto* for the period of the intervention and follow-up, and not *de jure*. This was, for example, the objective of the Paris Accords of 1991 on Cambodia, where the device of a "Supreme National Council" with representatives of the four competing factions, transferred effective authority to the UN to run the country until elections could be held. Similarly, Yugoslavia could be said to have temporarily had its sovereignty over Kosovo suspended, though it has not lost it *de jure*. The objective overall is not to change constitutional arrangements, but to protect them. As was noted in the discussion above of trusteeship, military intervention means endeavouring to sustain forms of government compatible with the sovereignty of the state in which the enforcement has occurred – not undermining that sovereignty.

Dependency and Distortion

5.27   A poorly administered occupation which overtly treats the people, or causes them to believe they are being treated, as an "enemy" will obviously be inimical to the success of any long-term rehabilitation efforts. Equally, a reconstruction and rehabilitation programme which does not take sufficient account of local priorities and excludes local personnel could create an unhealthy dependency on the intervening authority, stultify the regrowth of local institutions and the economy, and infinitely delay the population's desire or ability to resume responsibility for its own government.

5.28   Although largely unavoidable, the sudden influx of large sums of foreign currencies that usually accompany an intervening military force (and subsequent police and administration personnel) can have highly distorting economic effects on often fragile economies, and create unrealistic expectations in at least parts of the population. In some cases, local elites may seek to profit from this situation and set up corrupt networks and practices. They are then likely to oppose early withdrawal of the intervening authority, while at the same time undermining any hopes for a successful economic and political rehabilitation of the country.

5.29   A further negative feature relates to the intervening authorities themselves. The longer a follow-up period continues, the greater the financial and material drain it may prove to be on the intervening states, unless they are among the richer developed countries. Even then, follow-up with no light at the end of the tunnel may prove to be a major disincentive for such countries to become involved in future exercises of the responsibility to protect, regardless of how worthy they might be. The balance to be struck between the long-term interests of the people and country where the intervention takes place and those of the interveners themselves can end up being a fine one.

Achieving Local Ownership

5.30   As the case of Kosovo demonstrates, it is essential to strike a balance between the responsibilities of international and local actors. International actors have the resources to help provide a secure environment and to begin the reconstruction process. But international authorities must take care not to confiscate or monopolize political responsibility on the ground. They must take steps to set up a political process between the conflicting parties and ethnic groups in a post-conflict society that develops local political competence within a framework that encourages cooperation between former antagonists. Without such a political process, and the transfer of responsibility from international to local agents, there is a substantial risk, first, that ethnic hostility within the territory will settle back into old patterns of hatred, and second, that local actors will sit back and let the international actors take all the responsibility for mediating local tensions.

5.31   The long-term aim of international actors in a post-conflict situation is "to do themselves out of a job." They can do this by creating political processes which require local actors to take over responsibility both for rebuilding their society and for creating patterns of cooperation between antagonistic groups. This process of devolving responsibility back to the local community is essential to maintaining the legitimacy of intervention itself. Intervening to protect human beings must not be tainted by any suspicion that is a form of neo-colonial imperialism. On the contrary, the responsibility to rebuild, which derives from the obligation to react, must be directed towards returning the society in question to those who live in it, and who, in the last instance, must take responsibility together for its future destiny.

6. THE QUESTION
OF AUTHORITY

6.1   There is an international responsibility to protect populations at risk, and this Commission has argued that it extends to a responsibility to *react* by appropriate means if catastrophe is occurring, or seems imminent. In extreme cases, that responsibility to react includes military intervention within a state, to carry out that human protection. We have spelled out in Chapter 4 the tough threshold and precautionary criteria that must be satisfied in these cases: just cause, right intention, last resort, proportional means and reasonable prospects. The criteria have to be tough, because the action proposed is itself extreme: military intervention means not only an intrusion into a sovereign state, but an intrusion involving the use of deadly force, on a potentially massive scale. But whose right is it to determine, in any particular case, whether a military intervention for human protection purposes should go ahead?

SOURCES OF AUTHORITY UNDER THE UN CHARTER

6.2   The bedrock non-intervention principle is spelt out in Article 2.4 of the Charter, which provides that "All Members shall refrain … from the threat or use of force against the territorial integrity or political independence of any state, or in any other manner inconsistent with the Purposes of the United Nations," and in Article 2.7 which prohibits the United Nations from intervening "in matters which are essentially within the domestic jurisdiction of any state." What lies "essentially within the domestic jurisdiction" is not further defined and is indeed much contested, especially in the context of human rights issues.

6.3   A crucial qualification to the bedrock principle is Article 24 of the Charter, which "to ensure prompt and effective action by the United Nations" confers upon the Security Council the "primary responsibility for the maintenance of international peace and security." There are important provisions relating to the pacific settlement of disputes in Chapter VI of the Charter, but the cutting edge of that responsibility is set out in Chapter VII, which describes the action the Security Council may take when it "determine[s] the existence of any threat to the peace, breach of the peace, or act of aggression" (Article 39) . Such action may fall short of the use of force, and consist of such measures as embargoes, sanctions and the severance of diplomatic relations (Article 41). However, should the Council consider that such measures are likely to be inadequate, "it may take such action by air, sea or land forces as may be necessary to maintain or restore international peace and security" – in other words, it may resort to or permit the use of military force (Article 42).

6.4   There is one other provision in the Charter expressly permitting the application of cross-border military force, Article 51, which acknowledges "the inherent right of individual or collective self-defence if an armed attack occurs against a Member of the UN" (it being also provided that the measures taken be immediately reported to the Security Council). This is unlikely to have application to the military intervention situations with which this report is concerned, other than for regional organizations acting with respect to one of their member states. This provision, and the Security Council authorization of coercion under the general provisions of Chapter VII, but nothing else in the Charter, expressly trump the domestic jurisdiction restriction.

6.5   Chapter VIII acknowledges the existence and security role of regional and sub-regional organizations, but expressly states that "no enforcement action shall be taken under regional arrangements or by regional agencies without the authorization of the Security Council." It is interesting to note, however, that in some cases that authorization has been after the event, as with the approval of the interventions by ECOWAS's Monitoring Group (ECOMOG) in Liberia in 1992 and Sierra Leone in 1997.

6.6   The general provisions of Chapter VII, the specific authorization of self-defence action in Article 51, and the provisions of Chapter VIII, together constitute a formidable source of authority to deal with security threats of all types. After the terrorist attacks of 11 September 2001, for example, the Security Council (calling in aid both Article 51 and Chapter VII generally), was quick to call for action in response – as was the General Assembly. The world already has in place a standing military and diplomatic organization with the capacity (if not always the will) to deal with the whole spectrum of peace, security and human protection issues: we call it the United Nations.

6.7   The Security Council has the "primary" but not the sole or exclusive responsibility under the Charter for peace and security matters. Article 10 gives a general responsibility to the UN General Assembly with regard to any matter within the scope of UN authority, and Article 11 gives the General Assembly a fallback responsibility with regard specifically to the maintenance of international peace and security – albeit only to make recommendations, not binding decisions. The only caveat, meant to prevent a split between the UN's two major organs, is that the Security Council must not be discussing that issue at the same time (Article 12). To these Charter bases for General Assembly action must be added the "Uniting for Peace" resolution of 1950, creating an Emergency Special Session procedure that was used as the basis for operations in Korea that year and subsequently in Egypt in 1956 and the Congo in 1960. It is evident that, even in the absence of Security Council endorsement and with the General Assembly's power only recommendatory, an intervention which took place with the backing of a two-thirds vote in the General Assembly would clearly have powerful moral and political support.

6.8   The UN, whatever arguments may persist about the meaning and scope of various Charter provisions, is unquestionably the principal institution for building, consolidating and using the authority of the international community. It was set up to be the linchpin of order and stability, the framework within which members of the international system negotiated agreements on the rules of behaviour and the legal norms of proper conduct in order to preserve the society of states. Thus simultaneously the UN was to be the forum for mediating power relationships; for accomplishing political change that is held to be just and desirable by the international community; for promulgating new norms; and for conferring the stamp of collective legitimacy.

6.9   The authority of the UN is underpinned not by coercive power, but by its role as the applicator of legitimacy. The concept of legitimacy acts as the connecting link between the exercise of authority and the recourse to power. Attempts to enforce authority can only be made by the legitimate agents of that authority. Collective intervention blessed by the UN is regarded as legitimate because it is duly authorized by a representative international body; unilateral intervention is seen as illegitimate because self-interested. Those who challenge or evade the authority of the UN as the sole legitimate guardian of international peace and security in specific instances run the risk of eroding its authority in general and also undermining the principle of a world order based on international law and universal norms.

6.10   The UN is also the symbol of what member states must *not* do. In the field of state–citizen relations, the totality of Charter clauses and instruments like the Universal Declaration of Human Rights restrict the authority of states to cause harm to their own people within territorial borders. In the sphere of military action across territorial borders, UN membership imposes the obligation on the major powers to refrain from unilateral intervention in favour of collectively authorized international intervention.

6.11   The responsibility for protecting the lives and promoting the welfare of citizens lies first and foremost with the sovereign state, secondly with domestic authorities acting in partnership with external actors, and only thirdly with international organizations. As we suggested in Chapter 2, in addressing the concept of sovereignty as responsibility, a crucial justification for vesting sovereignty in the state derives from this principle. There is a gap – a responsibility deficit – if the state proves unable or unwilling to protect citizens, or itself becomes the perpetrator of violence against its own citizens.

6.12   The community-sanctioning authority to settle issues of international peace and security has been transferred from the great powers in concert to the UN. The UN, with the Security Council at the heart of the international law-enforcement system, is the only organization with universally accepted authority to validate such operations. But it does not by itself have any operational capacity. For the UN to function effectively as a law-enforcing collective security organization, states must renounce the unilateral use of force for national purposes. But the corollary, not always as readily accepted, is that states should be willing to use force on behalf of, as directed by, and for the goals of the UN.

THE SECURITY COUNCIL'S ROLE – AND RESPONSIBILITY

6.13   Because the prohibitions and presumptions against intervention are so explicitly spelled out in the Charter, and since no "humanitarian exception" to these prohibitions is explicitly provided for, the role of the Security Council becomes of paramount importance. There are a number of questions that can reasonably be asked about its authority and credibility, and we address them below: its legal capacity to authorize military intervention operations; its political will to do so, and generally uneven performance; its unrepresentative membership; and its inherent institutional double standards with the Permanent Five veto power. There are many reasons for being dissatisfied with the role that the Security Council has played so far.

6.14   But all that said, the Commission is in absolutely no doubt that there is no better or more appropriate body than the Security Council to deal with military intervention issues for human protection purposes. It is the Security Council which should be making the hard decisions in the hard cases about overriding state sovereignty. And it is the Security Council which should be making the often even harder decisions to mobilize effective resources, including military resources, to rescue populations at risk when there is no serious opposition on sovereignty grounds. That was the overwhelming consensus we found in all our consultations around the world. If international consensus is ever to be reached about when, where, how and by whom military intervention should happen, it is very clear that the central role of the Security Council will have to be at the heart of that consensus. The task is not to find alternatives to the Security Council as a source of authority, but to make the Security Council work much better than it has.

6.15 It is a necessary corollary of this perception of the Security Council's role that it be established as a matter of practice that all proposals for military intervention be formally brought before it. The Commission accordingly is agreed that:

❑ Security Council authorization must in all cases be sought prior to any military intervention action being carried out. Those calling for an intervention must formally request such authorization, or have the Council raise the matter on its own initiative, or have the Secretary-General raise it under Article 99 of the UN Charter; and

❑ The Security Council should deal promptly with any request for authority to intervene where there are allegations of large scale loss of human life or ethnic cleansing; it should in this context seek adequate verification of facts or conditions on the ground that might support a military intervention.

Legal Capacity

6.16 Article 42 authorizes the Security Council, in the event that non-military measures prove "inadequate," to decide upon military measures "as may be necessary" "to maintain or restore international peace and security." Although these powers were interpreted narrowly during the Cold War, since then the Security Council has taken a very expansive view as to what constitutes "international peace and security" for this purpose, and in practice an authorization by the Security Council has almost invariably been universally accepted as conferring international legality on an action. The cross-border implications of a number of the interventions authorized in the post-Cold War years have not been in doubt. But there is equally no doubt that in other cases – Somalia most prominent among them – the cross-border implications were less evident.

6.17 It is arguable that what the Security Council has really been doing in these cases is giving credence to what we described in Chapter 2 as the emerging guiding principle of the "responsibility to protect," a principle grounded in a miscellany of legal foundations (human rights treaty provisions, the Genocide Convention, Geneva Conventions, International Criminal Court statute and the like), growing state practice – and the Security Council's own practice. If such a reliance continues in the future, it may eventually be that a new rule of customary international law to this effect comes to be recognized, but as we have already acknowledged it would be quite premature to make any claim about the existence now of such a rule.

6.18 An important unresolved theoretical question is whether the Security Council can in fact exceed its own authority by violating the constitutional restraints embedded in the Charter, particularly the inhibition in Article 2.7. This issue has only been tangentially considered by the International Court of Justice (ICJ) in the *Lockerbie* case, with the 1998 decision on preliminary objections affirming that the Security Council is bound by the Charter. But the issue seems destined to remain a theoretical one, since there is no provision for judicial review of Security Council decisions, and therefore no way that a dispute over Charter interpretation can be resolved. It appears that the Council will continue to have considerable latitude to define the scope of what constitutes a threat to international peace and security.

Legitimacy and the Veto

6.19 A common theme in a great many of the Commission's consultations was the democratic legitimacy of the fifteen-member Security Council, which can hardly claim to be representative of the realities of the modern era so long as it excludes from permanent membership countries of major size and influence, in particular from Africa, Asia and Latin America. The Security Council was also variously claimed to be neither answerable to the peoples of the world, nor accountable to the plenary General Assembly nor subject to juridical supervision and scrutiny. There is no doubt that reform of the Security Council, in particular to broaden and make more genuinely representative its composition, would help in building its credibility and authority – though not necessarily making the decision making process any easier. But this is not a debate into which this Commission need enter for the purposes of this report.

6.20 An issue which we cannot avoid addressing, however, is that of the veto power enjoyed by the present Permanent Five. Many of our interlocutors regarded capricious use of the veto, or threat of its use, as likely to be the principal obstacle to effective international action in cases where quick and decisive action is needed to stop or avert a significant humanitarian crisis. As has been said, it is unconscionable that one veto can override the rest of humanity on matters of grave humanitarian concern. Of particular concern is the possibility that needed action will be held hostage to unrelated concerns of one or more of the permanent members – a situation that has too frequently occurred in the past. There is another political problem. Those states who insist on the right to retaining permanent membership of the UN Security Council and the resulting veto power, are in a difficult position when they claim to be entitled to act outside the UN framework as a result of the Council being paralyzed by a veto cast by another permanent member. That is, those who insist on keeping the existing rules of the game unchanged have a correspondingly less compelling claim to rejecting any specific outcome when the game is played by those very rules.

6.21 For all these reasons, the Commission supports the proposal put to us in an exploratory way by a senior representative of one of the Permanent Five countries, that there be agreed by the Permanent Five a "code of conduct" for the use of the veto with respect to actions that are needed to stop or avert a significant humanitarian crisis. The idea essentially is that a permanent member, in matters where its vital national interests were not claimed to be involved, would not use its veto to obstruct the passage of what would otherwise be a majority resolution. The expression "constructive abstention" has been used in this context in the past. It is unrealistic to imagine any amendment of the Charter happening any time soon so far as the veto power and its distribution are concerned. But the adoption by the permanent members of a more formal, mutually agreed practice to govern these situations in the future would be a very healthy development.

Political Will and Performance

6.22 The Commission recalls the Secretary-General's warning that "If the collective conscience of humanity … cannot find in the United Nations its greatest tribune, there is a grave danger that it will look elsewhere for peace and for justice." If the Council – and the five permanent members in particular – fail to make the Council relevant to the critical issues of the day then they can only expect that the Council will diminish in significance, stature and authority.

6.23   While the Council has from time to time demonstrated a commitment and a capacity to fulfill this responsibility, too often it has fallen short of its responsibilities, or failed to live up to expectations. Sometimes this has been the result of a sheer lack of interest on the part of the five permanent members. Sometimes it has been because of anxiety about how a particular commitment would play in domestic politics. Often in the past, it has been the result of disagreements among the five permanent members on what if any action should be taken. Increasingly, it has resulted from a reluctance on the part of some key members to bear the burdens – especially the financial and personnel burdens – of international action.

6.24   It is especially important that every effort be made to encourage the Security Council to exercise – and not abdicate – its responsibility to protect. This means, as Article 24 of the Charter requires, prompt and effective engagement by the Council when matters of international peace and security are directly at issue. And it means clear and responsible leadership by the Council especially when significant loss of human life is occurring or is threatened, even though there may be no direct or imminent threat to international peace and security in the strict sense.

6.25   The UN exists in a world of sovereign states, and its operations must be based in political realism. But the organization is also the repository of international idealism, and that sense is fundamental to its identity. It is still the main focus of the hopes and aspirations for a future where men and women live at peace with each other and in harmony with nature. The reality of human insecurity cannot simply be wished away. Yet the idea of a universal organization dedicated to protecting peace and promoting welfare – of achieving a better life in a safer world, for all – survived the death, destruction and disillusionment of armed conflicts, genocide, persistent poverty, environmental degradation and the many assaults on human dignity of the 20th century.

6.26   For the UN to succeed, the world community must match the demands made on the organization by the resources given to it. The UN has the moral legitimacy, political credibility and administrative impartiality to mediate, moderate and reconcile the competing pulls and tensions that still plague international relations. People continue to look to the UN to guide and protect them when the tasks are too big and complex for nations and regions to handle by themselves. The comparative advantages of the UN are its universal membership, political legitimacy, administrative impartiality, technical expertise, convening and mobilizing power, and dedication of its staff.

6.27   The UN represents the idea that unbridled nationalism and the raw interplay of power must be mediated and moderated in an international framework. It is the centre for harmonizing national interests and forging the international interest. Only the UN can authorize military action on behalf of the entire international community, instead of a select few. But the UN does not have its own military and police forces, and a multinational coalition of allies can offer a more credible and efficient military force when robust action is needed and warranted. What will be increasingly needed in the future are partnerships of the able, the willing and the well-intended – and the duly authorized.

WHEN THE SECURITY COUNCIL FAILS TO ACT

6.28   We have made abundantly clear our view that the Security Council should be the first port of call on any matter relating to military intervention for human protection purposes. But the question remains whether it should be the last. In view of the Council's past inability or unwillingness to fulfill the role expected of it, if the Security Council expressly rejects a proposal for intervention where humanitarian or human rights issues are significantly at stake, or the Council fails to deal with such a proposal within a reasonable time, it is difficult to argue that alternative means of discharging the responsibility to protect can be entirely discounted. What are the options in this respect?

The General Assembly

6.29   One possible alternative, for which we found significant support in a number of our consultations, would be to seek support for military action from the General Assembly meeting in an Emergency Special Session under the established "Uniting for Peace" procedures. These were developed in 1950 specifically to address the situation where the Security Council, because of lack of unanimity of the permanent members, fails to exercise its primary responsibility for the maintenance of international peace and security. Since speed will often be of the essence, it is provided that an Emergency Special Session must not only be convened within 24 hours of the request being made, but must also, under Rule of Procedure 65 of the General Assembly, "convene in plenary session only and proceed directly to consider the item proposed for consideration in the request for the holding of the session, without previous reference to the General Committee or to any other Committee."

6.30   Although the General Assembly lacks the power to direct that action be taken, a decision by the General Assembly in favour of action, if supported by an overwhelming majority of member states, would provide a high degree of legitimacy for an intervention which subsequently took place, and encourage the Security Council to rethink its position. The practical difficulty in all of this is to contemplate the unlikelihood, in any but very exceptional case, of a two-thirds majority, as required under the Uniting for Peace procedure, being able to be put together in a political environment in which there has been either no majority on the Security Council, or a veto imposed or threatened by one or more permanent members – although Kosovo and Rwanda might just conceivably have been such cases. The Commission believes, nonetheless, that the mere possibility that this action might be taken will be an important additional form of leverage on the Security Council to encourage it to act decisively and appropriately.

Regional Organizations

6.31   A further possibility would be for collective intervention to be pursued by a regional or sub-regional organization acting within its defining boundaries. Many human catastrophes will have significant direct effects on neighbouring countries through spill-over across national borders taking such forms as refugee flows or use of territory as a base by rebel groups. Such neighbouring states will thus usually have a strong collective interest, only part of which will be motivated by humanitarian concerns, for dealing swiftly and effectively with the catastrophe. It has long been acknowledged that neighbouring states acting within the framework of regional or sub-regional organizations are often (but not always) better placed to act than the UN, and Article 52 of the Charter has been interpreted as giving them considerable flexibility in this respect.

6.32   It is generally the case that countries within the region are more sensitive to the issues and context behind the conflict headlines, more familiar with the actors and personalities involved in the conflict, and have a greater stake in overseeing a return to peace and prosperity. All this should facilitate mobilizing the necessary will for fulfilling the responsibility to protect and for ensuring sustainability and follow-up.

6.33   All that said, organizations with a comprehensive regional membership have generally not displayed a notable zeal for intervening in the affairs of member states. An inhibiting consideration always is the fear that the tiger of intervention, once let loose, may turn on the rider: today's intervener could become the object of tomorrow's intervention. The numerical majority of any collective organization, almost by definition, will be the smaller, less powerful states, suspicious of the motives of the most powerful in their midst, and reluctant to sanction interference by the powerful against fellow-weaklings. In Africa and, to a lesser extent, the Americas, however, there has been acceptance of the right of regional and sub-regional organizations to take action, including military action, against members in certain circumstances. The OAU has set up a mechanism for the prevention, management and resolution of conflict, extending thereby its ability to deal with such situations.

6.34   It is much more controversial when a regional organization acts, not against a member or within its area of membership, but against a non-member. This was a large factor in the criticism of NATO's action in Kosovo since it was outside NATO's area. NATO argues, nevertheless, that the conflict in Kosovo had the potential to spill over NATO borders and cause severe disruption, and was thus a matter of direct concern to it. Other regional and sub-regional organizations which have mounted military operations have acted strictly within their geographical boundaries against member states.

6.35   The UN Charter recognizes legitimate roles for regional organizations and regional arrangements in Chapter VIII. In strict terms, as we have already noted, the letter of the Charter requires action by regional organizations always to be subject to prior authorization from the Security Council. But as we have also noted, there are recent cases when approval has been sought *ex post facto*, or after the event (Liberia and Sierra Leone), and there may be certain leeway for future action in this regard.

The Implications of Inaction

6.36   Interventions by ad hoc coalitions (or, even more, individual states) acting without the approval of the Security Council, or the General Assembly, or a regional or sub-regional grouping of which the target state is a member, do not – it would be an understatement to say – find wide favour. Even those countries involved in the Kosovo intervention, and prepared to passionately defend its legitimacy by reference to all the threshold and precautionary criteria we have identified in this report, for the most part acknowledge its highly exceptional character, and express the view that it would have been much preferable to have secured the Security Council's – or failing that the General Assembly's – endorsement. One view that has some currency is that an *ex post facto* authorization, of the kind that has occurred for the African regional instances mentioned above, might conceivably have been obtained in the Kosovo and Rwanda cases, and may offer a way out of the dilemma should any such case occur again in the future.

6.37   As a matter of political reality, it would be impossible to find consensus, in the Commission's view, around any set of proposals for military intervention which acknowledged the validity of any intervention not authorized by the Security Council or General

Assembly. But that may still leave circumstances when the Security Council fails to discharge what this Commission would regard as its responsibility to protect, in a conscience-shocking situation crying out for action. It is a real question in these circumstances where lies the most harm: in the damage to international order if the Security Council is bypassed or in the damage to that order if human beings are slaughtered while the Security Council stands by.

6.38   In the view of the Commission, there are two important messages for the Security Council in all of this.

6.39   The first message is that if the Security Council fails to discharge its responsibility in conscience-shocking situations crying out for action, then it is unrealistic to expect that concerned states will rule out other means and forms of action to meet the gravity and urgency of these situations. If collective organizations will not authorize collective intervention against regimes that flout the most elementary norms of legitimate governmental behaviour, then the pressures for intervention by ad hoc coalitions or individual states will surely intensify. And there is a risk then that such interventions, without the discipline and constraints of UN authorization, will not be conducted for the right reasons or with the right commitment to the necessary precautionary principles.

6.40   The second message is that if, following the failure of the Council to act, a military intervention is undertaken by an ad hoc coalition or individual state which *does* fully observe and respect all the criteria we have identified, and if that intervention is carried through successfully – and is seen by world public opinion to have been carried through successfully – then this may have enduringly serious consequences for the stature and credibility of the UN itself.

7. THE OPERATIONAL DIMENSION

7.1   Military interventions for human protection purposes have different objectives than both traditional warfighting and traditional peacekeeping operations. Such interventions therefore raise a number of new, different and unique operational challenges. Because the objective of military intervention is to protect populations and not to defeat or destroy an enemy militarily, it differs from traditional warfighting. While military intervention operations require the use of as much force as is necessary, which may on occasion be a great deal, to protect the population at risk, their basic objective is always to achieve quick success with as little cost as possible in civilian lives and inflicting as little damage as possible so as to enhance recovery prospects in the post-conflict phase. In warfighting, by contrast, the neutralization of an opponent's military or industrial capabilities is often the instrument to force surrender.

7.2   On the other hand, military intervention operations – which have to do whatever it takes to meet their responsibility to protect – will have to be able and willing to engage in much more robust action than is permitted by traditional peacekeeping, where the core task is the monitoring, supervision and verification of ceasefires and peace agreements, and where the emphasis has always been on consent, neutrality and the non-use of force. The *Panel on United Nations Peace Operations* compiled in 2000 a thorough review of the operational challenges facing United Nations military missions, but for the most part that panel focused on traditional peacekeeping and its variations, not the more robust use of military force – not least because there is not within UN headquarters the kind of logistic planning and support, and command and control capacity, that would make possible either warfighting or military interventions of any significant size. Their report confirmed that "the United Nations does not wage war. Where enforcement action is required, it has consistently been entrusted to coalitions of willing states."

7.3   The context in which intervention operations take place also has important operational significance. Military intervention to protect endangered human lives should and will occur only as a last resort, after the failure of other measures to achieve satisfactory results. Inevitably, it will be part of a broader political strategy directed towards persuading the targeted state to cooperate with international efforts. The consequences for such operations suggest that the specific nature of the task to protect may over time lead to the evolution of a new type of military operation, carried out in new ways.

PREVENTIVE OPERATIONS

7.4   There are two distinct categories of preventive military operations, with quite distinct characteristics. The first is "preventive deployment," which involves the positioning of troops where there is an emerging threat of conflict, with the consent of the government or governments concerned, for the primary purpose of deterring the escalation of that situation into armed conflict. The deterrent lies not in the military capability of the force but in the interest the Security Council has shown by authorizing the deployment, the placing of relevant parties under close international scrutiny, and the implication of willingness by the international community to take further action if there is a resort to violence.

7.5   The main example of such a deployment was UNPREDEP in Macedonia, from 1992 until its untimely withdrawal in 1999. While the essential purpose of this deployment was to deter any possible hostility from Yugoslavia, it has been argued – perhaps with too much benefit of hindsight – that the presence of the force also had a stabilizing influence on the fragile internal situation. The operational problems confronting any such deployment are essentially the same as those involved for a traditional UN peacekeeping operation.

7.6   The second category of preventive operation is where military resources are deployed without an actual intervention on the territory of the targeted state, and accordingly the question of consent does not arise. Such operations may be intended as a show of force to give added weight to diplomatic initiatives, or perhaps serve as instruments to monitor or implement non-military enforcement actions such as sanctions and embargoes, including in humanitarian crisis situations. The rules of engagement for such operations will primarily be of a defensive nature, and only to a very limited degree, if at all, allow forcing an opponent to comply. Preventive military action in this sense can be important in providing a firewall to try to help keep a conflict in a neighbouring country from spreading. A robust and decisive deployment may help to deter trouble, but can also provide a rapid response capacity should trouble arise.

7.7   If prevention in either of these categories fails altogether, the preventive operation may need to be turned into an intervention tool. Such forces should therefore be deployed and equipped for preventive operations in such a way that they could easily be designated as part of an intervention force.

PLANNING FOR MILITARY INTERVENTION

7.8   If a military intervention is to be contemplated, careful advance planning is a prerequisite for success. There are many challenges to be surmounted, including the need to build an effective political coalition, work out agreed objectives, provide a clear mandate, devise a common plan of operations, and marshal the necessary resources. Especially important to bear in mind is that the intervention phase is only one element in a broader political effort, and it must operate in harmony with these broader objectives. The military intervention phase will necessarily be preceded by preventive actions which may themselves include military measures such as sanctions or embargo enforcement, preventive deployments, or no-fly zones. The military intervention phase will likely be followed by post-conflict operations – discussed further below – which in most cases will include the deployment of peacekeeping forces for often substantial periods of time. The operational concept for an operation to protect needs therefore to provide a smooth transition from pre-intervention efforts to post-intervention activities.

Coalition Building

7.9   Most interventions have involved in the past, and are likely to in the future, multinational coalition operations. The cohesion of an intervening coalition – politically and militarily – is critical to the prospects for success, and the fragility of the intervening coalition has thus been one of the most vulnerable aspects of past interventions. It has been observed that coalition operations will necessarily be characterized by gradualism and possibly delays in striking sensitive targets, and that these are lasting military disadvantages of coalition operations that are only partly compensated by the stronger political impact of such operations in comparison with those of a single country. Spoilers have been ready to target the unity of the coalition directly in order to neutralize the international presence or cause its withdrawal.

7.10 At times, the weakness of the coalition and the failure to establish authority and to provide a secure environment have also led to the institution of parallel enforcement missions in the middle of a process – such as the arrival of the Unified Task Force (UNITAF) amidst the first UN Operation in Somalia (UNOSOM I), NATO's insertion of a rapid-reaction and bombing capacity amidst the UN Protection Force in the Former Yugoslavia (UNPROFOR), and more recently the British Army in Sierra Leone.

7.11 Effective coalition building means creating and maintaining a common political resolve, and working out a common military approach. Enforcement actions conducted by coalitions of the willing have to take into account the politics of member states and the impact of the media. Politics always intrudes on military efforts, and this situation is intensified when the military operation is not a classic war making effort. The intervention by NATO in Kosovo demonstrated that the pace and intensity of military operations may be seriously affected by the lowest common political denominator among member states. Moreover, coalition warfare entails other restrictions on military conduct and political decision making that results from differing national legislation.

7.12 Even where there is a common political resolve among coalition partners, it is still necessary for there to be a common military approach. A situation in which different militaries acted independently and without coordination would be one extreme, and the result would likely be failure. But even among well disciplined coalitions, important differences may arise that can have significant operational consequences. Differences have emerged in the past, for example, on whether some military options (for instance, the use of ground troops, to take but one well known example) should publicly be ruled out or not. Ruling in or out particular military options can have important political ramifications as well, and in some cases may even strengthen the resolve of the targeted state to resist.

Objectives

7.13 The effort to build broad support for an intervention action often confronts the problem that coalition partners may well have different ideas about the objectives to be achieved through the intervention action. Ideally, the process of making a decision to intervene, the formulation of the mandate for the intervening agent (or combination of agents), and the allocation of structures and means for implementation should be related. But harmonizing the views and interests of differing states in each regard is often a protracted and complex undertaking. Moreover, multilateral decision making bodies require consensus to succeed, and vagueness and incrementalism, rather than specificity, are inevitable outcomes of multilateral deliberations: the limits and boundaries of intervention may become significantly obscured in order to secure agreement about an authorization.

7.14 Differences in objectives often emerge in discussions over the "exit strategy," with some partners emphasizing the need to address the underlying problems, and others focusing on the earliest possible withdrawal. How an intervention will ultimately play out is always hard to determine. Unexpected challenges are almost certain to arise, and the results are almost always different from what was envisaged at the outset. In addition, many military operations begin with fairly simple and straightforward goals, only to have them expanded to the pursuit of military, political, and developmental objectives as operational circumstances change or as new peace agreements and deals are struck. Yet, mission creep has been the rule, not the exception. This uncertainty is what drives some intervening countries and their militaries to define an exit strategy in terms of an arbitrary withdrawal date.

Mandate

7.15 A clear and unambiguous mandate is one of the first and most important requirements of an operation to protect. However well or ill-defined the end state of intervention, political vision should encompass what it will take to get there – conceptually, as well as in terms of resources. Without such calculations from the outset, a problem of mustering sufficient "political will" to see the intervention through to a successful conclusion exists. All too often, this vision has been limited to a commitment to verify, monitor, and report on circumstances in the mission area. Comprehensive and multidimensional peace processes militate against a stricter focus on the art of the possible during cease-fire and peace negotiations. Considerable issues of prestige are at stake in an intervention, which translates into reluctance among potential contributors to support a coalition that is tasked with a challenging mandate, especially where vital interests are not regarded as being engaged.

7.16 The objective of the mandate should be to allow the executing military commander to identify his mission and his tasks properly and to propose an operational concept which promises quick success, paramount for an operation which aims at the protection of humans under attack. This will allow the commander to propose the size and composition of the necessary forces and to draft appropriate rules of engagement (ROEs) and to ask for political authorization and the allocation of the resources necessary to mount and to sustain the operation.

7.17 Mandates are often adjusted incrementally in reaction to new demands during the course of an intervention, and this may well be inevitable given the special nature of interventions for human protection purposes where much depends upon the attitude and level of cooperation received from the targeted state. While the initial mandate may reflect a preoccupation with human protection, political and security concerns sooner or later predominate. The more limited the initial vision in relation to the real problem at hand, the more likely that mission creep will take place. Somalia is a clear example where the initial response to insecurity and famine was not also accompanied by sufficient support to achieve long-term solutions. The follow-on UN operation (UNOSOM II) included ambitious security and political tasks but without commensurate means to realize them. However, the mandate should define in clear language what the aims of the intervention in the various phases of it would be and it should spell out that the desired end state is the restoration of good governance and the rule of law.

Resources and Commitment

7.18 Any operation to protect in response to large scale humanitarian threat or emergency requires that the countries, as well as the relevant international organizations involved, be prepared to sustain the operation with the resources required. The allocation of sufficient resources is indispensable for success, and failure to do so has been a major problem in the past.

7.19 The level of resources committed sends a clear signal of resolve and intent to all concerned. In the case of operations mounted by developing countries and their regional organizations especially, the sustainability of such operations may well be a significant and ongoing concern. Without broader international support, few developing countries are likely to be in a position to make a long-term military commitment to an intervention – a circumstance that could lead to the premature withdrawal of such forces before all important human protection objectives have been secured.

CARRYING OUT MILITARY INTERVENTION

Command Structure

7.20 Military decision making is based on clear and unequivocal communications and chains of command, and unity of command is essential for the successful conduct of operations. It is achieved best if there is a single chain of integrated command and if nations are prepared to transfer the authority over the forces they contribute to the fullest extent possible to the force commander they appointed to execute the intervention. The differing national interests of the intervening nations and the legal differences which exist due to different national laws will likely result in some limitations with respect to the degree to which forces will be placed under the command of the officer charged to conduct the intervention operation, and with respect to the use of deadly force. However, the fewer the national reservations on the employment of the national contingents in such an operation are, the greater is the capacity of the force commander to act decisively and flexibly.

7.21 Tight political control of such operations is mandatory, but political control does not mean micro-management of military operations by political authorities. Political leaders need to set clear objectives for each phase, within defined operational parameters. Military commanders should carry out these objectives, seeking further guidance when the objectives have been completed, or significant new challenges arise.

Civil–Military Relations

7.22 Where military intervention is required, the intervening military forces, civilian authorities (local and external), and humanitarian organizations are likely to be working side-by-side to bring assistance and protection to populations at risk. The coming together of the more hierarchical and disciplined military and the more diffuse humanitarian cultures in particular has sometimes been a source of significant tension. Improved coordination and collaboration between military forces, political civilian authorities, and humanitarian agencies will likely continue to be an issue of particular significance.

7.23 When enforcement begins, there are humanitarian consequences and tough choices about short- and long-term trade-offs. Even in the most insecure and unstable of circumstances, dedicated humanitarian organizations remain as long as possible. That the staff of the ICRC remained in Kigali as UN soldiers departed, or that numerous NGOs remained in Sarajevo despite snipers and rocket attacks, suggests the commitment by civilians to providing assistance and protection to affected local populations.

7.24 Yet, in seeking to apply deadly force, militaries may make it impossible for humanitarian workers to remain. Less humanitarian assistance in the short-run may be required in order to improve security and, ultimately, humanitarian action in the longer-run. For instance, Bosnia demonstrated that "lift and strike" was incompatible with continued humanitarian operations. The same would have been true had it actually been possible to undertake disarming the massive refugee camps controlled by *génocidaires* in Eastern Zaire. Outside humanitarians would have been forced to abandon the camps while the mopping-up occurred. Aid workers (as is the case with journalists) can become pawns and hostages.

7.25   Coordination is a topic that is a perpetual concern but which is extremely difficult to achieve satisfactorily, since coordination implies independent authorities attempting to cooperate with each other. Often, coordination does not translate into integrated decision making on a regular basis, nor to genuine unity of effort. While coordination efforts have markedly improved effectiveness in some cases, in others they have amounted to little more than trying to minimize turf wars.

Rules of Engagement

7.26   ROEs are critical to responding and protecting populations at risk. They are the directions guiding the application of the use of force by soldiers in the theatre of operations. The ROEs must fit the operational concept and be appropriate for the type of military action that is anticipated. The use of only minimal force in self-defence that characterizes traditional peacekeeping would clearly be inappropriate and inadequate for a peace enforcement action, including a military intervention. Activities such as arresting criminals (in the streets or indicted war criminals), halting abuse, and deterring would-be killers and thugs require clear and robust rules of engagement. Precise ROEs can help to diminish the need for individual countries to issue additional clarifications – something that can be a significant impediment to the conduct of multinational operations.

7.27   The rules of engagement should also reflect the principle of proportionality. Proportionality in this context ought not to exclude the option to escalate as appropriate, but should lead to restraint in the use of destructive power of modern weaponry. Proportionality should also not have the effect of paralyzing the military forces on the ground, or trap them into a purely reactive mode denying them the opportunity to seize the initiative when this may be needed.

7.28   In the context of interventions undertaken for human protection purposes, the ROEs for a military intervention must reflect a stringent observance of international law, and international humanitarian law in particular. They should include an acknowledgement that certain types of arms, and particularly those which are banned under international agreements, may not be used.

7.29   There is no common disciplinary procedure for international troops that violate international norms. It is largely left to contributing nations to prosecute their own soldiers, including with regard to their behaviour in respect of the civilian population in the place of operations. Particular care must be taken by intervening nations to establish codes of conduct and to ensure justice and accountability in the exercise of these responsibilities, so as not to discredit an intervening force in the eyes of a local population and undermine civilian attempts to establish a rule of law. The standards set by such codes should be high, and those who do not live up to them should be removed.

Applying Force

7.30   Quick success in military operations can best be achieved by surprise, by applying overwhelming force and through the concentration of all military efforts. However, it has been observed that in the context of an intervention for human protection purposes, it will be virtually impossible to rely on secrecy and surprise or to make maximum use of the full and devastating power of modern weapons. Achieving surprise at the strategic level must be balanced against the value and need to try to persuade the target state to comply before the resort to force is required. Moreover, democratic societies that are sensitive to human rights and the rule of law will not long tolerate the pervasive use of overwhelming military power.

7.31   Military planners will wish to compensate for the lost option of strategic surprise by resorting to a concentrated use of the military power at their disposal. Political circumstances and the conditions on the ground may or may not permit this. A critical factor which will impact on the intensity of operations, is the need for cooperation from the civilian population once the immediate objective of stopping the killing or ethnic cleansing has been achieved. This means first and foremost not to conduct military actions which will result in widespread hatred against the intervening nations. To win the hearts and minds of the people under attack is presumably impossible during the attack but planning has to be done in such a way that not all doors will be closed when the armed conflict comes to an end. This means accepting limitations and demonstrating through the use of restraint that the operation is not a war to defeat a state but an operation to protect populations in that state from being harassed, persecuted or killed. Taking these considerations into account means accepting some incrementalism as far as the intensity of operations is concerned, and some gradualism with regard to the phases of an operation and the selection of targets. Such an approach may also be the only way to keep the military coalition together. While this is a clear violation of the principles which govern war operations, one has to keep in mind that operations to protect are operations other than war.

7.32   To compensate to some extent for these disadvantages, the planning stages of an intervention – to reinforce the point we made at the outset of this chapter – must be especially focused. Means should be carefully tailored to objectives, and the key military and political pressure points identified and targeted. The roles of non-military components should be planned for and taken into account. Possible contingencies should be studied and contingency plans drawn up.

Casualties

7.33   Often, modalities for the proactive use of force have been determined more by military expediency than by any sense of responsibility to protect humanitarian interests. In Bosnia, for example, those advocating military intervention typically used its feasibility – meaning air strikes without casualties – as their prime argument, not moral or legal or operational obligations. They rarely admitted the considerable risks to the intervening force associated with effective intervention. The real question, ultimately, was whether the West was willing to risk the lives of its soldiers in order to stop war crimes, human rights abuse, and forced migration.

7.34   Force protection of the intervening force is important, but should never be allowed to become the principal objective. Where force protection becomes the prime concern, withdrawal – perhaps followed by a new and more robust initiative – may be the best course.

Media Relations

7.35   The omnipresent media and the worldwide near real time coverage of military operations will expose everyone who uses overwhelming military power too excessively to worldwide criticism. In operations other than self-defence such use of military power will reduce the degree of public support for military operations which is the more needed the less the average person on the street understands why his or her country had to intervene.

7.36   Modern communications and media coverage also have an impact on enforcement in that there is a new capacity for the public to monitor the impact of military action on civilians. Enforcement is likely to receive widespread public support if deadly force is applied in a way that can, if not approved, at least be tolerated by the majority of the populations in the countries of a coalition. The media coverage of civilian suffering as a result of sanctions in Iraq or of airstrikes in Serbia is a new element in determining military as well as political strategies.

7.37   Therefore, operational planning for an operation to protect should contain a fairly detailed sub-concept for public information. Proper conduct of an appropriate public information campaign is not only critical to maintaining public support for an intervention but also to maintaining the cohesion of the coalition. The difficulty in designing this concept will be to reconcile the requirements of accurate, comprehensive and fast information with the necessities of operational security. The cohesion of the intervening coalition and the desirability of eroding to the extent possible the support the opposing leader may enjoy with his or her own people or with allies, are of crucial importance. In these circumstances, there should be no doubt that in contrast to war or enforcement operations information will have priority over operational security, although the chances to achieve surprises will thus be further reduced.

FOLLOWING UP MILITARY INTERVENTION

Transfer of Authority

7.38   The main mission of military forces in post-intervention operations is to provide the safe environment necessary for the restoration of good governance and the rule of law. Additionally military forces may have to assist in reconstruction in areas which are too dangerous for non-military personnel to enter. The conduct of such operations means often that the forces will increasingly have to do what under normal circumstances police would do, at least initially. In addition, the forces have to be prepared to enforce compliance and, if necessary, to defend the country.

7.39   These tasks are more complex and cover a wider range than combat operations normally do. The chain of command will be increasingly blurred since civilian authorities will often take the lead on the ground. There is a need for clear-cut responsibilities and a transition of responsibility from the military authorities to the civilian authorities, as soon as possible after hostilities have ceased. While it may be necessary for a short period immediately after hostilities have ceased for the military commander to assume complete administrative authority, the transition to civilian authority should take place with minimum delay. The usual process will be the appointment by the UN of a Special Representative of the Secretary-General, and the transfer of military authority to that Special Representative, with full local authority restored following elections and the withdrawal of foreign military forces.

Peacekeeping and Peace Building

7.40   To see an intervention through means as well that the intervening side has to be prepared to remain engaged during the post-intervention phase as long as necessary in order to achieve self-sustained stability. Coalitions or nations act irresponsibly if they intervene without the will to restore peace and stability, and to sustain a post-intervention operation for as long as necessary to do so.

7.41   Past experience demonstrates that, if the internal security challenge is not handled early, "old" habits and structures will prevail and undermine other efforts to enhance post-conflict peace building. The immediate aftermath of any civil war spawns organized crime, revenge attacks, arms proliferation, looting and theft. UN civilian police officers deployed alongside peacekeepers, in order to assist in the resuscitation of national law enforcement agencies, have not been equipped to address the issue of law enforcement in a "not crime–not war" environment. The military has remained the only viable instrument although this reality has been obscured by the notion of peace as the antithesis of war.

Five Protection Tasks

7.42 Five analytically distinct kinds of protection tasks that emerge from these post-enforcement experiences are worth highlighting here. The first is the protection of minorities. This operational challenge is particularly important when civilians return to territories where another ethnic group is in the majority. The Balkans have provided numerous examples of the difficulties, and the relatively low number of refugees and IDPs who have returned is telling.

7.43 The second major protection task is security sector reform. The focus of such tasks has been to assist local authorities in their own process of security sector transformation. Bilateral and multilateral donors alike have sought to influence the direction of change, establish good practices, and transfer knowledge and insights to the new authorities. The importance as well as the difficulty of such efforts to recruit and train local police and reform the penal and judiciary systems have been evident in countries as diverse as Haiti, Rwanda and East Timor. The problems are especially difficult in situations where trained personnel have been killed or fled in large numbers to avoid violence.

7.44 In this respect, an interim challenge concerns the use of civilian police. In fact, civilian police now number second only to soldiers in UN operations. In light of the post-war conflicts and need for impartiality, the need for civilian police operations dealing with intra-state conflict is likely to remain a high priority in helping war-torn societies restore conditions for social, economic and political stability. The difficulty of recruiting international police is a central and crucial constraint, particularly in light of the need to reform and restructure local police forces in addition to advising, training, and monitoring new recruits.

7.45 The third main task is disarmament, demobilization, and reintegration. Although reintegration is key to longer-term peace building, and ultimately the resumption of the path to economic and social development, the focus here is on the security and protection of civilians. As reflected in Security Council resolutions and mission mandates, the key to stabilization has always been the demobilization of former combatants. The unstated purpose of stabilization measures has been to wrest power and the means of violence from local militias and warlords and to re-centralize it at a much higher level. In other words, the success of the whole intervention process has hinged on the degree to which warring factions can be effectively disarmed. However, disarmament has been one of the most difficult tasks to implement. It has been extremely hard to collect all weapons, even at the end of an armed struggle, when the remaining conditions of insecurity create high incentives for the maintenance and acquisition of light weapons and small arms by the community at large. Physical security and economic needs fuel a trade in small arms long after the withdrawal of intervention forces.

7.46 All disarmament commitments in peace processes have tended, at least at the outset, to be based on consent – regardless of whether the external forces deploy under a Chapter VI or VII mandate. However, the idea of voluntary disarmament is soon challenged by issues such as the security and economic livelihood of combatants thinking about turning in their weapons, along with the normally insufficient number of peace support forces. Faced with non-compliance with the disarmament provisions of the mandate, intervention forces have exhibited two basic reactions. The first is international acquiescence in the face of local recalcitrance, combined with a shift in the mandate that allows the "peace process" to proceed regardless. The second approach has been to apply limited coercion to recalcitrant parties, while attempting to preserve the consensual nature of the intervention at the strategic level.

7.47 Cambodia and Angola provide classic examples of the acquiescent approach, while Somalia and, to an extent, Bosnia are examples of attempted coercion. Regional and UN operations in West Africa have been characterized by a perplexing admixture of coercion and acquiescence, while the approach to disarmament and security challenges in Rwanda defies logic. None of these examples, however, can provide positive conclusions about the ability of intervening military forces to improve the protection of civilians at risk by reducing arms available to local soldiers, militias, and gangs. In fact, the cases of Somalia and Srebrenica have shown that, if this is not possible, it may be better not to pursue disarmament at all. Intervention forces with a disarmament mandate have not been provided with the doctrinal, political and military discretion to pursue a coercive strategy.

7.48 There is a fourth protection task which, with the growing universalization of the Ottawa Convention, is becoming a more common element of post-intervention, mandates: mine action. This means a range of activities from the effective marking of known or suspected anti-personnel minefields, to humanitarian mine clearance and victim assistance. The establishment of the United Nations Mine Action Service, the Geneva International Centre for Humanitarian Demining and the growing network of national Mine Action Centres is proving to be a successful model for coordinated mine action from donors to mine-affected countries. Recent experiences in operations such as Ethiopia/Eritrea, Cambodia and Kosovo have shown that early coordination of mine awareness training (often offered by military personnel) – with marking, mapping and clearance efforts (also often offered by those forces) – and the carefully planned, sequential return of refugees and IDPs, have resulted in far fewer mine casualties and victims than originally feared. Mine action integrated into post-conflict peace operations is recognized as an essential element in effective, sustainable economic and social reconstruction and rehabilitation efforts.

7.49 The fifth security task during the transition relates to the pursuit of war criminals. The details of the on-going criminal proceedings for the former Yugoslavia and for Rwanda have been analyzed earlier. What is worth mentioning here is the possible new demand on military and police forces during and following enforcement actions, especially once the International Criminal Court is established. NATO commanders and politicians have been hesitant to pursue and arrest indicted war criminals because of the possible hostility and violent reactions by local populations. Although some indicted criminals in the Balkans remain in hiding or are even allowed to live openly, this new operational challenge is likely to grow.

A DOCTRINE FOR HUMAN PROTECTION OPERATIONS

7.50 In summary, the responsibility to protect means that human protection operations will be different from both the traditional operational concepts for waging war and for UN peacekeeping operations. It would be advisable, accordingly, to embody the principles laid out in this Chapter, together with the guidance contained in Chapter 4, in a "Doctrine for Human Protection Operations." The Commission recommends to the UN Secretary-General that he take steps to initiate the development of such a doctrine. It would proceed from the fundamental thesis of this report that any coercive intervention for human protection purposes is but one element in a continuum of intervention, which begins with preventive efforts and ends with the responsibility to rebuild, so that respect for human life and the rule of law will be restored.

7.51 The doctrine should clearly be based on the following principles:

- ❑ the operation must be based on a precisely defined political objective expressed in a clear and unambiguous mandate, with matching resources and rules of engagement;

- ❑ the intervention must be politically controlled, but be conducted by a military commander with authority to command to the fullest extent possible, who disposes of adequate resources to execute his mission and with a single chain of command which reflects unity of command and purpose;

- ❑ the aim of the human protection operation is to enforce compliance with human rights and the rule of law as quickly and as comprehensively as possible, but it is not the defeat of a state; this must properly be reflected in the application of force, with limitations on the application of force having to be accepted, together with some incrementalism and gradualism tailored to the objective to protect;

- ❑ the conduct of the operation must guarantee maximum protection of all elements of the civilian population;

- ❑ strict adherence to international humanitarian law must be ensured;

- ❑ force protection for the intervening force must never have priority over the resolve to accomplish the mission; and

- ❑ there must be maximum coordination between military and civilian authorities and organizations.

8. THE RESPONSIBILITY TO PROTECT: THE WAY FORWARD

FROM ANALYSIS TO ACTION

8.1   This report has been about compelling human need, about populations at risk of slaughter, ethnic cleansing and starvation. It has been about the responsibility of sovereign states to protect their own people from such harm – and about the need for the larger international community to exercise that responsibility if states are unwilling or unable to do so themselves.

8.2   Past debates on intervention have tended to proceed as if intervention and state sovereignty were inherently contradictory and irreconcilable concepts – with support for one necessarily coming at the expense of the other. But in the course of our consultations this Commission has found less tension between these principles than we expected. We found broad willingness to accept the idea that the responsibility to protect its people from killing and other grave harm was the most basic and fundamental of all the responsibilities that sovereignty imposes – and that if a state cannot or will not protect its people from such harm, then coercive intervention for human protection purposes, including ultimately military intervention, by others in the international community may be warranted in extreme cases. We found broad support, in other words, for the core principle identified in this report, the idea of the responsibility to protect.

8.3   The most strongly expressed concerns that the Commission did hear in the course of our year-long consultations around the world went essentially to the political and operational consequences of reconciling the principle of shared responsibility with that of non-intervention. These concerns were of three different kinds. They might be described, respectively, as concerns about process, about priorities, and about delivery, with a cross-cutting concern about competent assessment of the need to act.

8.4   As to *process*, the main concern was to ensure that when protective action is taken, and in particular when there is military intervention for human protection purposes, it is under-taken in a way that reinforces the collective responsibility of the international community to address such issues, rather than allowing opportunities and excuses for unilateral action. The Commission has sought to address these concerns by focusing, above all, on the central role and responsibility of the United Nations Security Council to take whatever action is needed. We have made some suggestions as to what should happen if the Security Council will not act but the task, as we have seen it, has been not to find alternatives to the Security Council as a source of authority, but to make it work much better than it has.

8.5   As to *priorities*, the main concern was that attention in past debates and policy making had focused overwhelmingly on reaction to catastrophe – and in particular reaction by military intervention – rather than trying to ensure that the catastrophe did not happen in the first place. The Commission has tried to redress this imbalance by emphasizing over and again the integral importance of prevention in the intervention debate, and also by pointing out the need for a major focus on post-conflict peace building issues whenever military intervention is undertaken. We have argued that the responsibility to protect embraces not only the responsibility to react, but the responsibility to prevent, and the responsibility to rebuild.

8.6   As to *delivery*, we found the most widespread concern of all. There were too many occasions during the last decade when the Security Council, faced with conscience-shocking situations, failed to respond as it should have with timely authorization and support. And events during the 1990s demonstrated on too many occasions that even a decision by the Security Council to authorize international action to address situations of grave humanitarian concern was no guarantee that any action would be taken, or taken effectively. The Commission has been conscious of the need to get operational responses right, and part of our report has been devoted to identifying the principles and rules that should govern military interventions for human protection purposes.

8.7   But it is even more important to get the necessary political commitment right, and this is the issue on which we focus in this chapter. It remains the case that unless the political will can be mustered to act when action is called for, the debate about intervention for human protection purposes will largely be academic. The most compelling task now is to work to ensure that when the call goes out to the community of states for action, that call will be answered. There must never again be mass killing or ethnic cleansing. There must be no more Rwandas.

MOBILIZING DOMESTIC POLITICAL WILL

8.8   The key to mobilizing international support is to mobilize domestic support, or at least neutralize domestic opposition. How an issue will play at home – what support or opposition there will be for a particular intervention decision, given the significant human costs and financial costs that may be involved, and the domestic resources that may need to be reallocated – is always a factor in international decision making, although the extent to which the domestic factor comes into play does, however, vary considerably, country by country and case by case.

8.9   Contextual factors like size and power, geography, and the nature of the political institutions and culture of the country concerned are all important in this respect. Some countries are just more instinctively internationalist, and more reflexively inclined to respond to pleas for multilateral cooperation, than others: really major powers tend never to be as interested in multilateralism as middle powers and small powers, because they don't think they have to be. Geographic proximity comes into play, simply because what happens nearby is more likely to endanger nationals, to raise significant security concerns, and to result in refugees, economic disruptions and unwanted political spillovers – and to capture media attention and generate demands for action accordingly. By contrast, cultural affinity can mean particular concern for the plight of co-religionists, or fellow language speakers, even in small countries far away. Again, an extremely inward-looking political culture, by contrast, can find it hard to accommodate any external supporting role; many political systems disproportionately reward political actors whose focus and commitments are wholly domestic in character, leaving quite isolated those willing to stand up for international engagement.

8.10   Particular caution is also routinely to be expected from those countries in possession of the military, police, economic and other assets that are most in demand in implement-ing intervention mandates. Given the magnitude of continuing operations in the Balkans (more than 50,000 troops), as well as the shrinking military budgets of most countries in the post-Cold War era, there are real constraints on how much spare capacity exists to take on additional burdens. UN peacekeeping may have peaked in 1993 at 78,000 troops. But today, if both NATO and UN missions are included, the number of soldiers in international peace operations has soared by about 40 per cent to 108,000. Even states willing in principle to look at new foreign military commitments are being compelled to make choices about how to use limited and strained military capabilities.

8.11   In mobilizing political support for intervention for human protection purposes, as for anything else, a great deal comes down to the leadership of key individuals and organizations. Someone, somewhere has to pick up the case and run with it. Political leaders are crucial in this respect, but they are not the only actors: they are, for the most part, acutely responsive to the demands and pressures placed upon them by their various political constituencies, and the domestic media, and they are much influenced by what is put to them by their own bureaucracies. NGOs have a crucial and ever increasing role, in turn, in contributing information, arguments and energy to influencing the decision making process, addressing themselves both directly to policy makers and indirectly to those who, in turn, influence them. The institutional processes through which decisions are made will vary enormously from country to country, but there are always those who are more responsible than others and they have to be identified, informed, stimulated, challenged, and held to account: if everyone is responsible, then no one is actually responsible.

8.12   The trouble with most discussions of "political will" is that more time is spent lamenting its absence than on analyzing its ingredients, and working out how to use them in different contexts. To reduce the issue to its bare essentials, what is necessary is a good understanding of the relevant institutional processes, as just mentioned, and good arguments. What constitutes a good argument will obviously depend on the particular context. But it is not too much of an oversimplification to say that, in most political systems around the world, pleas for international action of the kind we are dealing with in this report need to be supported by arguments having four different kinds of appeal: moral, financial, national interest and partisan.

8.13   As to *moral* appeal, preventing, averting and halting human suffering – all the catastrophic loss and misery that go with slaughter and ethnic cleansing and mass starvation – are inspiring and legitimizing motives in almost any political environment. Political leaders often underestimate the sheer sense of decency and compassion that prevails in their electorates, at least when people's attention is engaged (just as they also underestimate the public willingness, when well informed, to accept the risk of casualties in well designed military interventions aimed at alleviating that suffering). Getting a moral motive to bite means, however, being able to convey a sense of urgency and reality about the threat to human life in a particular situation. Unfortunately, this is always harder to convey at the crucial stage of prevention than it is after some actual horror has occurred.

8.14   The best *financial* argument is that earlier action is always cheaper than later action. If prevention is possible, it is likely to be cheaper by many orders of magnitude than responding after the event through military action, humanitarian relief assistance, post-conflict reconstruction, or all three. In Kosovo, almost any kind of preventive activity – whether it involved more effective preventive diplomacy, or the earlier and sharper application of coercive preventive measures like the credible threat of ground-level military action – would have had to be cheaper than the $46 billion the international community is estimated to have committed at the time of writing in fighting the war and following up with peace-keeping and reconstruction.

8.15 *National interest* appeals can be made at many different levels. Avoiding the disintegration of a neighbour, with the refugee outflows and general regional security destabilization associated with it can be a compelling motive in many contexts. National economic interests often can be equally well served by keeping resource supply lines, trade routes and markets undisrupted. And whatever may have been the case in the past, these days peace is generally regarded as much better for business than war.

8.16 There is another dimension of the national interest which is highly relevant to intervention for human protection purposes: every country's national interest in being, and being seen to be, a good international citizen. There is much direct reciprocal benefit to be gained in an interdependent, globalized world where nobody can solve all their own problems: my country's assistance for you today in solving your neighbourhood refugee and terrorism problem, might reasonably lead you to be more willing to help solve my environmental or drugs problem tomorrow. The interest in being seen to be a good international citizen is simply the reputational benefit that a country can win for itself, over time, by being regularly willing to pitch into international tasks for motives that appear to be relatively selfless.

8.17 Making an argument with a *partisan* appeal for a government concerned about its political support at the ballot box or elsewhere is a more delicate matter. The point is simply that in any particular country, arguments which may not have a strong or sufficient appeal to the community at large may still have that appeal to a key section of the government's own particular support base, and be extremely influential for that reason. Governments often have to do things without knowing what is the majority view, and even when they know that the majority sentiment might be against the proposed action. What often matters more is that they have arguments that will appeal to, or at least not alienate, their immediate support base; and that they have arguments that they can use to deflate, or at least defend against, the attacks of their political opponents.

MOBILIZING INTERNATIONAL POLITICAL WILL

8.18 What happens in capitals is a crucial ingredient in international decision making. But it is only part of the story. International political will is more than just the sum of attitudes and policies of individual countries. What happens between states and their representatives in bilateral and multilateral contacts, and within intergovernmental organizations, is obviously also crucial. To get the right words uttered, and to turn them into deeds, requires – at international as at domestic level – the same kind of commitment and leadership, and the same kind of constant campaigning. Mobilizing support for specific instances of intervention is always a challenge, because there will always be a compelling rationale for inaction. The same strictures apply internationally as domestically about understanding where in the various processes responsibility for decision making actually lies, and how to pin it down. And it is just as important in the international arena as it is in the domestic to be able to produce arguments appealing to morality, resource concerns, institutional interests and political interests. This whole report is, in a sense, an expression of just such arguments in the context of intervention for human protection purposes.

8.19 An obvious starting point when looking for multilateral leadership on questions relating to intervention is the UN Secretary-General and senior officials in the Secretariat. Although the Secretary-General's formal role under Article 99 of the UN Charter could, as we have suggested, be further developed, his routine activities and interaction with the Security Council, and his international profile with governments and the media, give him a unique opportunity to mobilize international support; an important further part of his multilateral leadership role lies in constructing and maintaining the multinational coalitions which are an essential element in the contemporary implementation of UN-authorized peace operations. The Secretariat, particularly through its reports and recommendations to the Security Council, makes a major contribution to shaping the deliberations and determining the range of options considered. That contribution, it must be said again, can be negative as well as positive: Rwanda in 1994 involved a failure, not only by key member states, but in the leadership of the UN and in the effective functioning of the Secretariat as well.

8.20   Beyond the UN itself, including all the organs and agencies in the system beyond the Secretariat, there are multiple other international actors whose roles are immensely relevant to the intervention issue, in particular regional and sub-regional organizations, and international NGOs, and the media. We have mentioned the key institutional players throughout this report, and need not here do so again.

8.21   As to the media, there is no question that good reporting, well-argued opinion pieces and in particular real time transmission of images of suffering do generate both domestic and international pressure to act. The "CNN effect" can be almost irresistible, unbalanced in its impact though it may be, with similarly troubling crises not always receiving similar attention. On the other hand, by focusing attention on human suffering, media attention sometimes tends to divert policy makers from hard diplomatic and military decisions, with time pressures sometimes pushing them to become involved before serious analysis and planning can occur. That is perhaps a lesser sin than those of total inertia or excessive delay, but it can create problems nonetheless.

8.22   International NGOs have been significant advocates of cross-border human protection action, extending in some cases to military intervention, and their positive influence in stirring response – especially in the West – has been great. Yet they too, from the perspective of the decision makers they seek to influence, can have their limitations as advocates: they are seen often as lacking in policy making experience, frequently as unhelpfully divided over which precise policy course is optimal, and sometimes as reluctant publicly (as distinct from privately) to endorse coercive measures which may be necessary, but which are not easy for governments or intergovernmental institutions to deliver without overt support.

8.23   The goals of policy makers and humanitarian advocates are not so different from each other. Given that the application of deadly force should remain an option of last resort, there is still a range of choices between doing nothing and sending in the troops. There are always options to be considered before, during, and after lethal conflicts. Both policy makers and humanitarian advocates would like to see public policy succeed in tackling the most crucial issues of the day. One of the most pressing such issues is how to make good the responsibility to protect those facing the worst sort of horrors the contemporary world has to provide.

NEXT STEPS

8.24   The Commission's objective from the outset has been for our report to have a practical and concrete political impact, rather then simply provide additional stimulation to scholars and other commentators – though we hope to have done that as well. Consistent with our practical focus we have been mindful, throughout our work and consultations, of the need to ensure a solid foundation for the discussions that will take place at the United Nations and in other international forums after the presentation of the report, as well as within governments and among those who seek to influence them.

immediate hope is that by helping to clarify and focus the terms of the debate –
ntest between sovereignty and intervention, but as involving "the responsibility to
s a common theme – a way forward will be found through the current polemics
ent impasse in that debate. We want, above all, to strengthen the prospects for
g action, on a collective and principled basis, with a minimum of double standards,
in response to conscience-shocking situations of great humanitarian need crying out for that
action. If our report can help to stimulate support for such action by reminding states of their
common responsibilities, then it will have made a very significant contribution indeed.

8.26 The principles of action around which we would like to see consensus develop are
summarized in the Synopsis set out in the first pages of this report. What should happen next
to advance them? There has been much discussion, at national, regional and international
levels, on how best to approach the practical task of trying to embody any new consensus
among states on the question of intervention for human protection purposes. Some suggest
that the focus should be on drafting guidelines for the internal use of the Security Council;
some support the passing of a more formal resolution by the General Assembly; and others
have gone so far as to suggest that work should begin on the drafting of a new international
convention, or even an amendment to the UN Charter itself.

8.27 The Commission believes that it would be premature to make a judgement now as
to what will ultimately prove possible if consensus around the idea of "the responsibility to
protect" builds to the extent that we hope it will. The important thing now is to make a start,
with member states working with the Secretary-General to give substantive and procedural
content to the ideas we advance. There are major roles to be played by the Secretary-General
himself, by the Security Council and by the General Assembly, and we make some suggestions in this respect in the following recommendations. The Commission makes no
judgement as to the most appropriate sequence in which these steps should be taken.

8.28 The Commission recommends to the General Assembly:

> That the General Assembly adopt a draft declaratory resolution embodying the
> basic principles of the responsibility to protect, and containing four basic elements:
>
> ❏ an affirmation of the idea of sovereignty as responsibility;
>
> ❏ an assertion of the threefold responsibility of the international community of states – to
> prevent, to react and to rebuild – when faced with human protection claims in states
> that are either unable or unwilling to discharge their responsibility to protect;
>
> ❏ a definition of the threshold (large scale loss of life or ethnic cleansing, actual or
> apprehended) which human protection claims must meet if they are to justify military
> intervention; and
>
> ❏ an articulation of the precautionary principles (right intention, last resort, proportional
> means and reasonable prospects) that must be observed when military force is used
> for human protection purposes.

8.29 The Commission recommends to the Security Council:

> (1) That the members of the Security Council should consider and seek to reach agreement
> on a set of guidelines, embracing the "Principles for Military Intervention" summarized
> in the Synopsis, to govern their responses to claims for military intervention for human
> protection purposes.

(2)   *That the Permanent Five members of the Security Council should consider and seek to reach agreement not to apply their veto power, in matters where their vital state interests are not involved, to obstruct the passage of resolutions authorizing military intervention for human protection purposes for which there is otherwise majority support.*

8.30   The Commission recommends to the Secretary-General:

That the Secretary-General give consideration, and consult as appropriate with the President of the Security Council and the President of the General Assembly, as to how the substance and action recommendations of this report can best be advanced in those two bodies, and by his own further action.

MEETING THE CHALLENGE

8.31   Throughout its deliberations, the Commission has sought to reconcile two objectives: to strengthen, not weaken, the sovereignty of states, and to improve the capacity of the international community to react decisively when states are either unable or unwilling to protect their own people. Reconciling these two objectives is essential. There is no prospect of genuine equality among peoples unless the sovereignty of states is respected and their capacity to protect their own citizens is enhanced. Equally, the very term "international community" will become a travesty unless the community of states can act decisively when large groups of human beings are being massacred or subjected to ethnic cleansing.

8.32   The Commission is optimistic that these dual objectives – enhancing the sovereign capacity of states and improving the ability of the international community to protect people in mortal danger – can be reconciled in practice. Our work reflects the remarkable, even historic, change that has occurred in the practice of states and the Security Council in the past generation. Thanks to this change, no one is prepared to defend the claim that states can do what they wish to their own people, and hide behind the principle of sovereignty in so doing. In the international community, just as there can be no impunity for unwarranted unilateral uses of force, nor can there be impunity for massacre and ethnic cleansing. No one who has perpetrated such horrors should ever be allowed to sleep easily.

8.33   This basic consensus implies that the international community has a responsibility to act decisively when states are unwilling or unable to fulfill these basic responsibilities. The Commission has sought to give clear articulation to this consensus, and calls on all members of the community of nations, together with non-governmental actors and citizens of states, to embrace the idea of the responsibility to protect as a basic element in the code of global citizenship, for states and peoples, in the 21st century.

8.34   Meeting this challenge is more than a matter of aspiration. It is a vital necessity. Nothing has done more harm to our shared ideal that we are all equal in worth and dignity, and that the earth is our common home, than the inability of the community of states to prevent genocide, massacre and ethnic cleansing. If we believe that all human beings are equally entitled to be protected from acts that shock the conscience of us all, then we must match rhetoric with reality, principle with practice. We cannot be content with reports and declarations. We must be prepared to act. We won't be able to live with ourselves if we do not.

APPENDIX A: MEMBERS OF THE COMMISSION

Gareth Evans *(Australia)*, *Co-Chair*, has been President and Chief Executive of the Brussels-based International Crisis Group since January 2000. He was an Australian Senator and MP from 1978 to 1999, and a Cabinet Minister for thirteen years (1983–96). As Foreign Minister (1988–96), he played prominent roles in developing the UN peace plan for Cambodia, concluding the Chemical Weapons Convention, founding the Asia Pacific Economic Cooperation (APEC) forum and initiating the Canberra Commission on the Elimination of Nuclear Weapons. He is a Queen's Counsel (1983), and Officer of the Order of Australia (2001). His many publications include *Cooperating for Peace* (1993) and the article "Cooperative Security and Intrastate Conflict" *(Foreign Policy*, 1994), for which he won the 1995 Grawemeyer Prize for Ideas Improving World Order.

Mohamed Sahnoun *(Algeria)*, *Co-Chair*, is a Special Advisor to the UN Secretary-General and has previously served as Special Envoy of the Secretary-General on the Ethiopian/Eritrean conflict (1999); Joint United Nations/Organization of African Unity (OAU) Special Representative for the Great Lakes of Africa (1997); and Special Representative of the Secretary-General for Somalia (March–October 1992). He was also a member of the World Commission on Environment and Development (the Brundtland Commission). A senior Algerian diplomat, he served as Ambassador to Germany, France, the United States, and Morocco, and as Permanent Representative to the United Nations in New York. He also served as Deputy Secretary-General of both the OAU and the Arab League.

Gisèle Côté-Harper *(Canada)* is a barrister and Professor of Law at Laval University, Quebec. She has been a member of, among numerous other bodies, the UN Human Rights Committee, the Inter-American Institute of Human Rights and the Quebec Human Rights Commission. She was Chair of the Board of the International Centre for Human Rights and Democratic Development (Montreal) in 1990–96 and a member of the official Canadian delegation to the Fourth World Conference on Women, Beijing 1995. She was awarded the Lester B. Pearson Peace Medal in 1995, and in 1997 became an Officer of the Order of Canada, as well as receiving the Quebec Bar Medal. Among her published works is *Traité de droit pénal canadien* (4th ed., 1998).

Lee Hamilton *(United States)* is Director of the Woodrow Wilson International Center for Scholars, Washington DC, and Director of the Center on Congress at Indiana University. A member of the US Congress from 1965 to 1999, his distinguished record includes Chairmanships of the Committee on International Relations, the Permanent Select Committee on Intelligence, and the Joint Economic Committee. He has served on a number of commissions dealing with international issues, including the Task Force on Strengthening Palestinian Public Institutions, the Task Force on the Future of International Financial Architecture, and the Council of Foreign Relations Independent Task Force on US–Cuban Relations in the 21st Century, as well as numerous other panels, committees and boards.

Michael Ignatieff *(Canada)* is currently Carr Professor of Human Rights Practice at the Kennedy School of Government, Harvard University. He is also a Senior Fellow of the 21st Century Trust, and served as a member of the Independent International Commission on Kosovo. Since 1984, he has worked as a freelance writer, broadcaster, historian, moral philosopher and cultural analyst. He has written extensively on ethnic conflict, and most recently on the various conflicts in the Balkans, including *Virtual War: Kosovo and Beyond*. He has also authored numerous other works, including a biography of the liberal philosopher Isaiah Berlin. *The Russian Album*, a family memoir, won Canada's Governor General's Literary Award and the Heinemann Prize of Britain's Royal Society of Literature in 1988. His second novel, *Scar Tissue*, was short-listed for the Booker Prize in 1993.

Vladimir Lukin *(Russia)* is currently Deputy Speaker of the Russian State Duma. He worked at the Institute of World Economics and International Relations, Moscow (1961–65) and the Institute of US and Canadian Studies of the USSR Academy of Sciences (1968–87). He also served from 1965–68 as an editor of the international journal *Problems of the World and Socialism* in Prague, but was expelled for opposing the Soviet invasion of Czechoslovakia in 1968. He joined the USSR Foreign Ministry in 1987 and served as Russian Ambassador to the USA (1992–93). He was elected a Deputy to the Supreme Soviet of the Russian Soviet Federated Socialist Republic in 1990 and to the State Duma of the Russian Federation in 1993. In that year he helped found the Yabloko Faction, a party which he still represents. He served as Chair of the International Affairs Committee of the Duma (1995–99).

Klaus Naumann *(Germany)* served as Chairman of the North Atlantic Military Committee of NATO (1996–99) and played a central role in managing the Kosovo crisis and in developing NATO's new integrated military command structure. He joined the German Bundeswehr in 1958. As a Colonel, he served on the staff of the German Military Representative to the NATO Military Committee in Brussels in 1981–82. He was promoted to Brigadier General in 1986, followed by a two-star assignment as Assistant Chief of Staff of the Federal Armed Forces. He was promoted to Four Star General in 1991 and appointed at the same time Chief of Staff, a position he held until becoming Chairman of the North Atlantic Military Committee. After retirement, he served as a member of the *Panel on United Nations Peace Operations*.

Cyril Ramaphosa *(South Africa)* is currently Executive Chairman of Rebserve, a major South African service and facilities management company. He was elected Secretary-General of the African National Congress in June 1991, but left politics for business in 1996. He played a major role in building the biggest and most powerful trade union in South Africa, the National Union of Mineworkers from 1982 onwards. A lawyer by training, his university years were interrupted by periods in jail for political activities. He played a crucial role in negotiations with the former South African regime to bring about a peaceful end to apartheid and steer the country towards its first democratic elections in April 1994, after which he was elected Chair of the new Constitutional Assembly. He received the Olaf Palme prize in October 1987 and was invited to participate in the Northern Ireland peace process in May 2000.

Fidel V. Ramos *(Philippines)* served as President of the Republic of the Philippines from 1992–98, and has, since 1999, been Chairman of the Ramos Peace and Development Foundation which deals with Asia Pacific security, sustainable development, democratic governance and economic diplomacy. Prior to becoming President, he had a long and distinguished military and police career, including service in both the Korean and Vietnam wars. He became Deputy Chief of Staff of the Armed Forces of the Philippines in 1981, and

Chief of Staff in 1986, and subsequently served as Secretary of National Defense from 1988–91. He played a central role in peace negotiations with Muslim rebels in the southern Philippines and wrote *Break Not the Peace*, a book about that peace process.

Cornelio Sommaruga *(Switzerland)* is currently President of the Caux Foundation for Moral Re-Armament as well as President of the Geneva International Centre for Humanitarian Demining. He is, in addition, a member of the Board of the Open Society Institute, Budapest and served as a member of the *Panel on United Nations Peace Operations*. Prior to that, he was President of the International Committee of the Red Cross (1987–99). From 1984 to 1986 he served as Switzerland's State Secretary for External Economic Affairs. From 1960, he had had a long and distinguished career as a Swiss diplomat, including a period from 1973 as Deputy Secretary-General of the European Free Trade Association (EFTA) in Geneva. In 1977–78 he served as President of the UN Economic Commission for Europe.

Eduardo Stein Barillas *(Guatemala)* is currently working with the United Nations Development Programme (UNDP) in Panama and served as Head of the Organization of American States (OAS) Observer Mission to Peru's May 2000 general elections. He was Guatemalan Foreign Minister (1996–2000), a position in which he played a key role in overseeing the Guatemalan peace negotiations, particularly in marshalling international support. He lectured in universities in Guatemala and Panama from 1971–80 and 1985–87, and from 1982 to 1993 was based in Panama and worked on various regional development projects within the Latin American Economic System (SELA) and the Contadora Group. This involved cooperation with various Latin American countries, the European Community and the Nordic countries. From December 1993 to 1995, he was Resident Representative in Panama of the International Organization for Migration.

Ramesh Thakur *(India)* has been Vice-Rector of the United Nations University, Tokyo, since 1998, in charge of the University's Peace and Governance Programme. Educated in India and Canada, he was a lecturer, then Professor of International Relations at the University of Otago (New Zealand) from 1980 to 1995. He was then appointed Professor and Head of the Peace Research Centre at the Australian National University in Canberra where he was involved in the Non-Proliferation Treaty Review and Extension Conference, drafting of the Comprehensive Test Ban Treaty and the International Campaign to Ban Landmines. He was also a consultant to the Canberra Commission on the Elimination of Nuclear Weapons. He is the author of numerous books and articles, including *Past Imperfect, Future Uncertain: The United Nations at Fifty*, and in 2000 co-edited *Kosovo and the Challenge of Humanitarian Intervention*.

APPENDIX B: HOW THE COMMISSION WORKED

Mandate

At the UN Millennium Assembly in September 2000, Canadian Prime Minister Jean Chrétien announced that an independent International Commission on Intervention and State Sovereignty (ICISS) would be established as a response to Secretary-General Kofi Annan's challenge to the international community to endeavour to build a new international consensus on how to respond in the face of massive violations of human rights and humanitarian law.

Launching the Commission on 14 September 2000, then Foreign Minister Lloyd Axworthy said that the mandate of the Commission would be to promote a comprehensive debate on the issues, and to foster global political consensus on how to move from polemics, and often paralysis, towards action within the international system, particularly through the United Nations. Much as the Brundtland Commission on Environment and Development in the 1980s took the apparently irreconcilable issues of development and environmental protection and, through the process of an intense intellectual and political debate, emerged with the notion of "sustainable development," it was hoped that ICISS would be able to find new ways of reconciling the seemingly irreconcilable notions of intervention and state sovereignty.

It was proposed that the Commission complete its work within a year, enabling the Canadian Government to take the opportunity of the 56th session of the United Nations General Assembly to inform the international community of the Commission's findings and recommendations for action.

Commissioners

The Canadian Government invited to head the Commission the Honourable Gareth Evans AO QC, President of the International Crisis Group and former Australian Foreign Minister, and His Excellency Mohamed Sahnoun of Algeria, Special Advisor to the UN Secretary-General and formerly his Special Representative for Somalia and the Great Lakes of Africa. In consultation with the Co-Chairs, ten other distinguished Commissioners were appointed, spanning between them an enormously diverse range of regional backgrounds, views and perspectives, and experiences, and eminently able to address the complex array of legal, moral, political and operational issues the Commission had to confront. A full list of members of the Commission, with biographical summaries, is contained in Appendix A.

Advisory Board

Canada's Minister of Foreign Affairs, the Honourable John Manley, appointed an international Advisory Board of serving and former foreign ministers and other eminent individuals to act as a political reference point for the ICISS. The Advisory Board was designed to help Commissioners ground their report in current political realities, and assist in building the political momentum and public engagement required to follow up its recommendations.

Members of the Advisory Board are the Honourable Lloyd Axworthy (Chair), Director and CEO of the Liu Centre for the Study of Global Issues at the University of British Columbia; Her Excellency María Soledad Alvear Valenzuela, Minister of Foreign Affairs of the Republic of Chile; Dr. Hanan Ashrawi, former Cabinet Minister of the Palestinian National Authority; Right Honourable Robin Cook, former British Foreign Secretary President of the Council and Leader of the House of Commons, United Kingdom of Great Britain and Northern Ireland; Mr. Jonathan F. Fanton, President of the John D. and Catherine T. MacArthur Foundation; Professor Bronisław Geremek, Chairman of the European Law Committee of the Sejm of the Republic of Poland; Her Excellency Rosario Green Macías, Former Secretary of Foreign Relations of the United Mexican States; Dr. Vartan Gregorian, President of Carnegie Corporation of New York; Dr. Ivan Head, Founding Director of the Liu Centre for the Study of Global Issues, University of British Columbia; Honorable Patrick Leahy, US Senator; His Excellency Amre Moussa, Secretary-General of the League of Arab States and former Minister of Foreign Affairs of the Arab Republic of Egypt; His Excellency George Papandreou, Minister of Foreign Affairs of the Hellenic Republic; His Excellency Dr. Surin Pitsuwan, former Minister of Foreign Affairs of the Kingdom of Thailand; Dr. Mamphela Ramphele, Managing Director of The World Bank Group and former Vice-Chancellor of the University of Cape Town; and His Excellency Adalberto Rodríguez Giavarini, Minister of Foreign Relations, International Trade and Worship of the Argentine Republic.

The Advisory Board met with Commissioners in London on 22 June 2001, with the following members participating in what proved to be a highly lively and productive debate: former Canadian Foreign Affairs Minister, Lloyd Axworthy; Secretary-General of the Arab League, Amre Moussa; former British Foreign Secretary, Robin Cook; former Mexican Foreign Minister, Rosario Green; former Chilean Foreign Minister Juan Gabriel Valdés (also representing the current Chilean Foreign Minister); representatives of the Foreign Ministers of Argentina and Greece; President of the MacArthur Foundation, Johnathan Fanton; and Founding Director of the Liu Centre at the University of British Columbia, Ivan Head.

Commission Meetings

Five full meetings of the Commission were held: in Ottawa on 5–6 November 2000; Maputo 11–12 March 2001; New Delhi 11–12 June 2001; Wakefield, Canada, 5–9 August 2001; and Brussels on 30 September 2001. There was also an informal Commission meeting in Geneva on 1 February 2001 involving a number of Commissioners in person and others by conference call, and multiple further meetings of small groups of Commissioners in the roundtables and consultations described below.

At their first meeting, Commissioners considered a series of central questions, identified the key issues and decided on a general approach. An early draft outline of the Report was then developed and circulated. This outline was considered at the Geneva meeting in early February, and expanded further at the Maputo meeting in March. A fuller draft was then produced in

May, circulated to Commissioners for consideration and initial comment, and considered in more detail at the New Delhi meeting in June. Significant changes to the substance and structure of the report were agreed at that meeting. On this basis, a further draft was produced and circulated in early July, with Commissioners making specific written comments.

The remaining stages of the process involved the Co-Chairs themselves – meeting in Brussels over several days in July – producing a further full-length draft, with substantial written input from a number of other Commissioners. The Co-Chairs' Draft, distributed to Commissioners a week in advance of the Commission meeting in Wakefield, was then considered in exhaustive detail over four days, with the terms of the report ultimately being agreed unanimously. A further meeting of the Commission was held in Brussels at the end of September to consider the implications for the report of the horrifying terrorist attacks on New York and Washington DC earlier that month: this resulted in a number of adjustments to the final text as published.

Consultation

In order to stimulate debate and ensure that the Commission heard the broadest possible range of views during the course of its mandate, eleven regional roundtables and national consultations were held around the world between January and July 2001. In date order, they were held in Ottawa on 15 January, Geneva on 30–31 January, London on 3 February, Maputo on 10 March, Washington, DC on 2 May, Santiago on 4 May, Cairo on 21 May, Paris on 23 May, New Delhi on 10 June, Beijing on 14 June and St Petersburg on 16 July. Summaries of the issues discussed in these meetings, and lists of those participating in them, may be found in the supplementary volume accompanying the Commission's report.

At least one, and usually both, of the Co-Chairs attended each of these consultations, for the most part with some other Commissioners as well. A variety of national and regional officials, and representatives of civil society, NGOs, academic institutions and think-tanks were invited to each of the meetings. A paper setting out the main issues from the Commission's perspective was circulated to participants in advance of the meetings to stimulate discussion, and specific participants were invited in advance to prepare papers and make special presentations on different aspects of the issues. These papers formed an additional and extremely useful source of research material on which the Commission could draw. A further participant at each roundtable was selected to produce a summary report of the proceedings and outcomes of each of the roundtables. These various contributions are more fully acknowledged in the supplementary volume to this report.

Regular briefings were also given to interested governments in capitals, as well as to diplomatic missions in Ottawa, Geneva and most recently in New York on 26–27 June, where the Commission met with representatives from a number of Permanent Missions as well as with Secretary-General Annan and key members of the UN Secretariat. Consultations were also held in Geneva on 31 January with the heads or senior representative of major international organisations (UN Office Geneva; UNHCR; Commission on Human Rights; WHO; IOM; ICRC/IFRCS; and OCHA).

Research

An extensive programme of research was organized in support of the Commission's work. Aiming to build upon and complement the many efforts previously undertaken on these issues, Commissioners drew upon the record of debate and discussion generated at the UN and in regional and other forums; the vast body of already published scholarly and policy research on this topic, including a number of important independent and nationally sponsored studies; and a series of papers and studies specially commissioned for the ICISS.

To supplement and consolidate the intellectual dimension of the Commission's work, an international research team was created. This was led jointly by Thomas G. Weiss of the United States, Presidential Professor at The Graduate Center of the City University of New York (CUNY) where he is also co-director of the UN Intellectual History Project, and Stanlake J.T.M. Samkange, of Zimbabwe, a lawyer and former speechwriter to UN Secretary-General Boutros Boutros-Ghali. Tom Weiss, with research consultant Don Hubert of Canada, assumed primary responsibility for producing the research papers contained in the supplementary volume, while Stanlake Samkange's primary role was as rapporteur, assisting the Commission in the drafting of its report.

Other members of the research team played important roles. Carolin Thielking at Oxford University, with supervision from Professor Neil MacFarlane, had a principal role in the preparation of the bibliography contained in the supplementary volume. The Research Directorate, located at the CUNY Graduate Center in New York, was also ably assisted by doctoral candidates Kevin Ozgercin and Peter Hoffman.

It is hoped that the research material prepared for the Commission and contained in the supplementary volume, together with the report itself, will constitute an enduring legacy for scholars, specialists and policy makers in the field. The supplementary volume, as well as the report, have accordingly been produced and made available in CD-ROM form, with the Bibliography cross-referenced with key-words to enhance its utility as a research tool. These and other documents also appear on the special ICISS web site – www.iciss-ciise.gc.ca – which will be maintained for at least the next five years.

Administrative Support

The workplan of the Commission was administered by a small Secretariat, provided as part of the Canadian government support for ICISS. Housed within the Department of Foreign Affairs and International Trade in Ottawa, the Secretariat undertook necessary fund-raising, organized the roundtable consultations and Commissioners' meetings, managed the publication and distribution of the Commission's report and background research, and spearheaded diplomatic efforts to engage governments and build political support for the debate. The Secretariat was led by Jill Sinclair, Executive Director, and Heidi Hulan, Deputy Director, and comprised Susan Finch, Manager of the Outreach Strategy; Tony Advokaat, Policy Advisor; Joseph Moffatt, Policy Advisor; Tudor Hera, Policy Analyst; Harriet Roos, Manager of Communications; and Carole Dupuis-Têtu, Administrative Assistant. Former Australian diplomat Ken Berry acted as Executive Assistant to the Co-Chairs, and staff at Canadian Embassies round the world and the International Development Research Centre (IDRC) in Ottawa provided additional support to the Secretariat.

Funding

ICISS was funded by the Canadian Government, together with major international foundations including the Carnegie Corporation of New York, the William and Flora Hewlett Foundation, the John D. and Catherine T. MacArthur Foundation, the Rockefeller Foundation, and the Simons Foundation. ICISS is also indebted to the Governments of Switzerland and the United Kingdom for their generous financial and in-kind support to the work of the Commission.

INDEX

A

academic institutions, 4
accountability, 13, 14, 19, 23, 51
actors, 3, 6, 25, 45, 70
ad hoc coalitions. *See* coalitions of the willing; Security
    Council — failure to act
administration under UN authority, **43**
Africa, 54
    Report on the Causes of Conflict and the Promotion of
        Durable Peace and Sustainable Development in, 40
Americas, 54
Amnesty International, 21
Angola, 66
Annan, Kofi, vii, 2, 15. *See also* United Nations: Secretary-
    General
arms control and disarmament, 23
attack on United States. *See* terrorism: attack on United States
authority, viii, 1, 5, 16, 53, **47–55**. *See also* Security Council
    ex post facto, **54**
    lack of, 16
    of intervening forces, 44, 59
    right, xi, 32, **47–55**
aviation bans, 30
Axworthy, Lloyd, ix

B

Belgium, 6, 24
blockades, 8
Bosnia, vii, 5, 20, 61, 63, 66
Brahimi Report. *See* Report of the Panel on United Nations
    Peace Operations
Bretton Woods institutions. *See* IMF, World Bank
Britain, 59

C

Cambodia, 20, 41, 44, 66
Canada, 2
capacity building, 22, 23, 26, 75
Carnegie Commission on the Prevention of Deadly
    Conflict, 20, 26
casualties. *See* operational issues
changing international environment. *See* intervention:
        changing environment
child soldiers, 4, 24
civilian – military relations. *See* operational issues
civilians as targets, 4, 13, 67
CNN effect. *See* media
coalition building, **58–59**
coalitions of the willing, 1, 52, 54, 57, 59, 73
Cold War, 50
    post-, 3, 4, 7, 71
    practice, 12
command structure. *See* operational issues
communications, improvements in. *See* globalization
conflict prevention. *See* prevention
conflict, intra-state, 4, 5, 13, 36, 65
Congo, 48

consistency, 5, 11, 42
constructive abstention. *See* veto power: code of conduct
Convention on the Prevention and Punishment of the Crime
        of Genocide. *See* Genocide Convention
crime, organized, 4, 5, 64
crimes against humanity, 6, 24, 33
criteria. *See* intervention: criteria for
Croatia, 42
cross-border raids, 12
customary international law, 6, 16, 50

D

debt relief, 20
decision to intervene. *See* intervention
demining. *See* operational issues: mine action
democracy, overthrow of, 34, 35
democratization, 4, 13, 23, 44
dependency on intervening forces. *See* rebuilding: dependency
development assistance, 19, **20**, 24
diamonds. *See* resources, capture of
diplomatic measures, 30, 47
direct prevention. *See* prevention: direct
disarmament, demobilization and reintegration. *See*
        operational issues.
discrimination – racial, religious, ethnic, 5
displaced persons, 40, 42, 65, 66
dissent, 16
    armed, 4
doctrine for human protection operations. *See* operational
        issues: proposed doctrine
domestic jurisdiction, 47
double standards, 24, 37, 49
drug trafficking, 4, 5, 30, 36

E

early warning, **21–22**
    creation of new unit, 22
East Timor, 37, 65
ECOMOG, 48
economic factors, 23, 24, 40, **42–43**, **70**, 72
ECOWAS, 16
Egypt, 48
El Salvador, 20
embargoes, 30, 58
emergency relief, 8
Emergency Special Session. *See* General Assembly; Uniting
        for Peace
emerging practice. *See* responsibility to protect
eminent persons commissions, 24
enforcement action. *See* peace enforcement
environmental catastrophes, 15, 33, 72
Eritrea, 66
Ethiopia, 66
ethnic cleansing, xi, xii, 5, 15, 31, **32–34**, 40, 71, 74, 75
evidence. *See* intervention: evidence
ex-combatants. *See* operational issues
exit strategy, 39, **41**, 59

The Publisher

The International Development Research Centre is a public corporation created by the Parliament of Canada in 1970 to help researchers and communities in the developing world find solutions to their social, economic, and environmental problems. Support is directed toward developing an indigenous research capacity to sustain policies and technologies developing countries need to build healthier, more equitable, and more prosperous societies.

IDRC Books publishes research results and scholarly studies on global and regional issues related to sustainable and equitable development. As a specialist in development literature, IDRC Books contributes to the body of knowledge on these issues to further the cause of global understanding and equity. IDRC publications are sold through its head office in Ottawa, Canada, as well as by IDRC's agents and distributors around the world. The full catalogue is available at http://www.idrc.ca/booktique/.